Three Circles

A practical guide to automatic enrolment

2nd Edition (January 2017)

Chris Daems

DEDICATION

This book is dedicated to everyone who's helped me write this book

They're too numerous to list here but include our clients, fellow professionals and my fantastic colleagues at both Cervello and AE in a Box.

This book is also dedicated to the three smart funny women I share my life with and without whom my life would be far poorer, Cassie, Charlotte and Sophie.

CONTENTS

Introduction

When I first published this book in November 2015 most employers were still yet to comply with automatic enrolment. In this second edition (published in January 2017) the reality is that despite hundreds of thousands of employers reaching their 'staging date' (the date employers need to comply with automatic enrolment by) the remaining employers who need to comply still outnumber the ones which have.

However automatic enrolment has changed since first publishing this book. Some of the rules have changed as well as the fact that the tools designed to help you comply have also improved.

The reality is that over the next couple of years if you're a business owner, business manager or work in a team where you're responsible for either payroll, pensions or HR you're going to be working to ensure your business complies with automatic enrolment regulation.

You see whilst automatic enrolment regulation is now just over 4 years old most employers still haven't complied with this significant change to their businesses. Change which will impact many of their internal business processes and may require significant action.

Many companies have already felt the impact of automatic enrolment. Organisations in a wide and diverse range of sectors from health care to transport, from supermarket chains to recruitment, all the way through to high street retailers have had to prepare, take action and continue to comply with automatic enrolment regulation.

However the reality is that most businesses, and more than likely your business as well as hundreds of thousands of businesses like yours, have yet to comply.

In fact between 2015 – 2018 the estimate is that 1.8 million medium and small employers in the UK who are yet to comply.

As I write this in January 2017 most employers have not complied yet with an estimated million employers who have yet to hit their staging date. This is in addition to the new businesses which have started to employer after 2012 who will need to comply with automatic enrolment over the next couple of years.

On page 8 you'll see a graph which highlights the number of employers who need to stage between 2015 and 2016 compared to the employers who have staged already.

This graph clearly illustrates one thing…

As I write this the automatic enrolment challenge for most employers is yet to come.

Therefore many small businesses in the UK have a significant challenge in the next few years.

You see whilst larger employers tend to have payroll departments, HR teams, financial directors and often pension departments the hundreds of thousands of businesses yet to comply have relatively limited resources.

Many smaller business usually have one individual who manages payroll, pensions and HR as well as having to manage daily operations within their businesses.

Also whilst larger businesses very often had significant budgets so they could appoint large teams of professionals with a deep understanding of all of the auto enrolment rules many smaller businesses don't have the capacity or wiliness to pay significant fees to get professional help to support them with the automatic enrolment challenge.

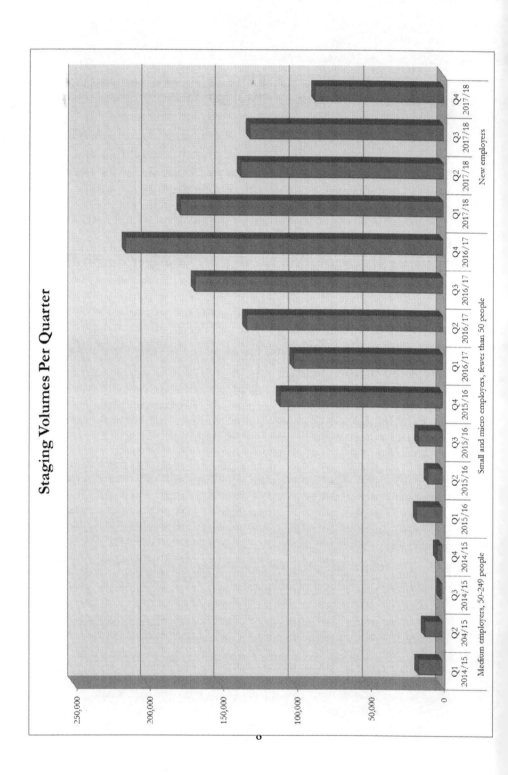

Over the past few years my team and I have helped numerous employers ranging from the relatively large (our largest client has been around 1,500 employees) to relatively small (our smallest employer has 14 employees) comply with auto enrolment regulation.

In partnership with the employers we've worked with, we've seen the impact of the new rules, faced many of the challenges and worked hand in hand with employers in aspects of their business as diverse as payroll, HR, communications and project management.

Also, with small and medium sized employers in mind I've been actively involved in developing an online system which helps support and guide employers through the initial steps they need to take and beyond[1]

So, in order to help as many small and medium sized businesses as I can I've decided to share my experience and knowledge in this book.

A book designed to help you navigate your businesses through the auto enrolment minefield and ensure that both its reputation remains intact and isn't impacted by the fines which can be levied on every business.

A book written in plain English where I've tried to take the complicated world of automatic enrolment and simplify it.

A book where I've tried to avoid technical terminology where possible and explained the journey to auto enrolment compliance in a straightforward step by step way.

A book which whilst not giving you all the answers, will provide you with many of the steps you need to take as well

---

[1] you can find out more about this particular system at www.aeinabox.co.uk

the decisions you need to make within your business to ensure you comply.

A book designed to support you as you help your business comply with auto enrolment.

So, this book is designed as a practical guide to help explain automatic enrolment and highlight the major considerations designed to help you comply successfully.

What this book isn't is a definitive guide to automatic enrolment regulation. There's a couple of reasons for this...

Firstly, if you're looking for clarification on every single niche, subtlety and angle of automatic enrolment regulation, the best place to look is the pension regulators website.

This book isn't designed to compete with what's provided on the pensions regulators webpages and within its detailed guidance (the place to go to confirm specific points on automatic enrolment regulation)

Instead I thought it would be more useful to compliment what's available from the regulator by making this book practical in nature and highlighting most of the clear actions you need to take to comply and provide clear signposts on where to get additional help and support.

Secondly, whilst we'll make every effort to ensure that this book is kept as up to date as possible if regulation changes we might not be able to practically update this book quickly enough to ensure it keeps up.

In fact when we originally published this book we were in a position where a few days after the launch event George Osborne (the then chancellor of the exchequer) stood up and made a change which meant a couple of pages contained in the first edition of this book were incorrect and therefore whilst I was slightly annoyed at the fact that Mr Osborne had changed one of the rules relating to automatic enrolment it did highlight the fact that regulation does change…and whilst we'll keep this book as up to date as possible and try to release future additions it's worth making sure you've got the most up to date copy.

However none of this means that this book won't continue to be useful as there's enough in here to ensure you take the right steps towards compliance.

It just means that you'll need to keep up to date with any changes which occur to the regulation, either using a support service or by constantly and consistently checking with the regulator on any changes which have occurred which might impact your business.

So, What's in this book?

Firstly, we're going to explore a little bit about the background of auto enrolment which will include an exploration on why this fundamental change in law is occurring.

We'll then explore the impact of auto enrolment and why this change might be fairly considered as one of the largest changes in not only pension but also employers legal obligations in decades and why the change isn't only pension related but also affects many of the core functions required to run a business including employment law and payroll.

We'll then look at the fact that, whilst new to you, automatic enrolment has been enshrined in law for some time and why this is important. Then we'll explore what the new regulations specifically mean to you and your business.

We'll also discuss the impact if you decide not to comply, something which will become almost immediately clear will be a potentially expensive mistake for any business.

We'll then look at why it's fundamentally important to have plenty of time to prepare before your businesses' 'staging date', why the key to successfully complying starts with a plan and the aspects which need to be included. This includes pensions, payroll, regulation and employment law.

Then we'll dig a bit deeper into the three primary aspects of complying with automatic enrolment it's vital to understand in order to comply successfully.

<u>Why this book is called "Three Circles"</u>

Over the past few years I've had the opportunity to talk to hundreds of financial advisers and planners, accountants, payroll bureaus, software businesses and most importantly employers.

During this time we've tried to continuously simplify and improve the way we explain the implications of automatic enrolment.

The reason I've called this book "Three Circles – A practical guide to auto enrolment" is that I've found the easiest way to explain the obligations an employer has under this regulation is to talk about these "Three circles".

Regulation, Pension and Payroll.

So, first we'll talk about the "circle of regulation" and what employers need to do under the new laws. We'll be providing practical step by step guidance in what you need to do in order to meet these new rules. Then we'll explain why complying with this new regulation starts but doesn't stop on the date you initially need to comply with automatic enrolment.

Then we'll explore the "circle of pensions" and talk about the questions you need to ask an existing pension provider (if your business already has a scheme in place) and provide some useful guidance on how to select a pension scheme.

Then we'll look at the "circle of payroll" and explain how important your payroll, and in particular your payroll software, is in the automatic enrolment process.

We'll discuss how payroll software can help you comply with the regulations and what you can do if it doesn't fulfil certain tasks. We'll also look at other options if your particular payroll software isn't up to the job.

Then we'll talk about what external support you can get and how this might help. Firstly we'll explore the help you can get from the professionals you work with, including your accountant, payroll firm or financial planner.

Whilst a professional can absolutely help you and your business comply with auto enrolment successfully it's important to ensure you're working with the right person or team. So we'll share with you the questions you should ask of any professional you choose to work with.

Then we'll look at some of the software tools available which will help support and guide you through your journey to compliance.

At the end of the book we'll explore how auto enrolment might change, share some practical case studies of how companies have successfully complied (by highlighting some of the challenges they have faced on the way) as well as providing you with a compendium of auto enrolment articles we've written.

In addition to this, and as I'm feeling extraordinarily generous, we'll also provide you with a template report you can use to help you plan your 'journey to automatic enrolment compliance' as well as an article to help you understand some of the wider employment law considerations which have an impact on your business.

Also, and due to the fact that employers need to consider the impact employment law has when complying with automatic enrolment legislation we've drafted in some expert help from Vandana Dass from Davenport Solicitors who at the back of the book has highlighted some of the things you need to consider in your business when drafting employment contracts and how this impacts your journey to automatic enrolment compliance.

I'll also share some stories, hopefully share some laughs (a tough challenge in a book about automatic enrolment but let's give it go shall we?) and more importantly provide you with the guidance you need to ensure your business complies successfully!

So, are you ready? Great! Let's begin....

Chapter 1

An introduction to Automatic Enrolment

Before we start talking about auto enrolment and commence exploring some of the background behind these rules let's answer an incredibly simple question.

What is auto enrolment?

Auto Enrolment is the name most commonly used for the rules which came into place in the (not so) snappily titled **Pensions Act 2008.**

The broad idea of auto enrolment is to ensure that more employees take greater control of their financial futures by saving for their 'retirement' into a pension scheme.

The responsibility for these rules doesn't sit with the employees but is firmly laid at the feet of the employer.

To comply with the new regulation employers broadly have to perform tasks in three main areas....

Payroll, Pensions and Regulation

We'll talk about some of the specific tasks, the categories they sit in and whether they fit firmly in one of the automatic enrolment 'circles' or straddle two or even three circles later in this book.

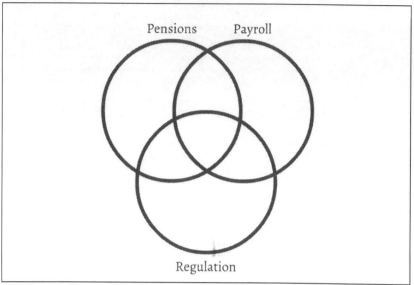

We've found that the easiest way to explain how payroll, pensions and regulatory tasks are related is to use a technique I've not personally used since secondary school…

The Venn Diagram!

As you can see from the diagram above, there are elements of automatic enrolment regulation which are pension, payroll and regulation related (if you hadn't guessed this is the 'three circles' of automatic enrolment.)

Some elements, as we've mentioned straddle two of the 'circles' and some elements relate to all three.

The elements of the new laws translate into one thing…

Tasks employers need to complete to comply.
Some of these tasks are a one off. Some of these tasks need to be completed on an ongoing basis.

Some of these tasks will need to be completed prior to your 'staging date' (for an explanation on this see the next page) and some need to be completed after.

Also, some tasks may change in the future as the regulation develops.

What's a staging date?

An employer's staging date is the date in which an employer needs to start to continuously comply with automatic enrolment.

However this doesn't mean that this is when an employer should start taking a look at their obligations as there's a bunch of preparation which needs to be done prior to this particular date.

Every employer in the UK has a staging date. It used to be based on the number of employees a particular business had.

However for smaller employers (less than 30 employees) it's based on the employer's PAYE reference number.

This means that since June 2015 you could employ two people (including you) or thirty and you might need to start to prepare sooner than you expect.

We've already had to help smaller clients who assumed that they had plenty of time to comply (due to being one of the smaller employers who has to comply with this legislation) and subsequently found out that they meet their obligations under the rules sooner rather than later (i.e. in 2015 instead of 2016 or 2017).

For employers who didn't have any employees prior to 2012 but now employ your staging date does depend on when you first started to employ staff.

The full details of when your staging date is likely to be is in the table below:-

Date PAYE income first payable	Staging date
Between 1 April 2012 and 31 March 2013	1 May 2017
Between 1 April 2013 and 31 March 2014	1 July 2017
Between 1 April 2014 and 31 March 2015	1 August 2017
Between 1 April 2015 and 31 December 2015	1 October 2017
Between 1 January 2016 and 30 September 2016	1 November 2017
Between 1 October 2016 and 30 June 2017	1 January 2018
Between 1 July 2017 and 30 September 2017	1 February 2018

This is why it's fundamentally important, instead of assuming you've got ages until your staging to ensure that the first thing you do as an employer is find out what your 'staging date' is although you may have already received a letter from The Pensions Regulator confirming your staging date.

However if you haven't received this letter or it's been mislaid and you don't know your businesses staging date let me suggest you find out now.

The easiest way of doing this is via The Pensions Regulator website.[2]

All sorted? Excellent! Let's move on…

But before we do it's important to mention that getting your staging date might not be as easy for the odd employer as checking the regulators website.

If you do get stuck let me suggest that you call the pension regulator directly who can highlight what the issue might be and point you in the right direction.

Why is auto enrolment being introduced?

Great question…thanks for asking it!

Now if I'm being entirely frank it's a question best answered by the politicians who bought it into law.

However there's a number of broad trends which provide an insight into why auto enrolment is now impacting millions of employers and tens of millions of employees across our green and pleasant land.

First, we're all living longer, relatively healthier lives.

A quick look at the trends on the office of national statistics website[3] tells an interesting story.

---

[2] To check your staging date go to
http://www.thepensionsregulator.gov.uk/employers/staging-date.aspx

[3] To have a look at trends of people living for longer go to
http://www.ons.gov.uk/ons/taxonomy/index.html?nscl=Life+Expectancies

We're living longer and the trend shows no indications of changing any time soon!

It's incredible to think that out of those born in 2013 the odds of living to 100 are now 1 in 3, something which was considered exceptional just a few short years ago.

Secondly many of us aren't saving enough for our retirement.

According to a report issued by Scottish Widows[4] in 2012 only 46% of us save sufficiently for our longer term financial futures. This leaves 54% of us where our retirements are looking increasingly bleak.

Thirdly, and due to the two factors we've already mentioned, the pressure on the state pension to deliver a decent income to all of us (as long as we've paid sufficient national insurance contributions of course) over the longer term has increased dramatically.

The History of Automatic Enrolment.

In the early part of the new millennium the wheels were put in motion to look at the changes which needed to be made to the current pension system in the UK.

This resulted, between 2004 and 2006 a number of reports being issued[5] by a commission let by Lord Adair Turner, into changes they felt should be made to the pension system in the UK to make it 'fit for purpose.'

---

[4]For Scottish Widows report on saving for the longer term financial future go to http://reference.scottishwidows.co.uk/docs/46273-2014.pdf

[5] For Lord Adair Turner's report on changes that should be made to the UK pension system go to http://www.webarchive.org.uk/wayback/archive/20070802120000/ http://www.pensionscommission.org.uk/index.html

These changes, broadly speaking, were designed to 'nudge' people into saving more for their financial futures by putting in place a number of laws which meant that employers had to put in place a pension, automatically enrol employees and explain the reasons why these rules were being implemented.

Many of the changes suggested were then bought into Law as part of the Pensions Act 2008.

Whilst a number of suggestions were made the one which was enshrined in law in 2008 and is due to impact hundreds of thousands of businesses over the next couple of years was, you guessed it, Automatic Enrolment.

So the combination of increased life expectancy, low levels of retirement saving and an increased pressure on the state has resulted in these new laws which mean that employers now need to put a pension in place, comply with a bunch of new laws and automatically enrol many of their employees into their workplace pension schemes.

These changes have been enshrined in law since 2008 and although there have been relatively slight changes to the regulation the reality remains that there's no sign that auto enrolment regulation is going anywhere soon.

The story since 2012

Whilst the regulation was established in 2008 the reality is that the first employers who had to comply were in 2012.

So in 2012 the first employers had to play ball and Automatic enrolment regulation impacted larger employers first.

Therefore a bunch of businesses including the large supermarket chains, sportswear firms and large manufacturing companies all had to take action to ensure they met with the new rules.

Once the larger employers in the country complied the medium sized firms had to meet their obligations under the new rules. Many of these firms had more significant challenges to face when compared to larger businesses.

Medium sized firms typically had less resources in order to comply. Large businesses usually have significant HR teams, payroll departments as well as the money to spend on solving their auto enrolment challenge. Medium sized businesses therefore had to solve the same problem with a reduced resource.

So far automatic enrolment, with the odd exception, has been a success. Almost all of the large and medium sized employers who needed to comply between 2012 and early 2015 complied successfully.

As I write this it's January 2017. This means we're sitting squarely in the middle of the period of time smaller businesses are complying with automatic enrolment and the picture is an interesting one.

Broadly speaking the story is a positive one. Most smaller businesses have complied with automatic enrolment successfully but before we start cracking open the champagne it's important we consider a couple of important factors…

There is always a significant delay in calculating how many firms are actually complying successfully.

This is in part due to how employers have 5 months to declare their compliance with the regulator (and therefore any vision of employer compliance being at least 5 months old) and the fact that the regulator reports how employers are doing every 3 months.

As I write this the latest regulator report came out in October which means that I'm writing about a picture of automatic enrolment compliance which is over 7 months old!

The reality is a true picture of whether automatic enrolment was successful will come out late in 2018 when the majority of employers have complied however it's worth sharing the updated statistics.

The reality is that compared to most large and medium sized businesses many more smaller businesses are failing to comply.

In total there have been nearly 35,000 employers who have received some form of enforcement notice or penalty just under 20,000 of these were between July 2016 – September 2016.

This means that 57% of the employers who have received some sort of enforcement notice or penalty have received it got it over the last 3 measured months!

Without being cynical I'd suspect that when the October to December 2016 statistics are released the trend for non-compliance will continue to expand.

So, whilst the majority of employers continue to comply successfully there is a growing trend showing that smaller businesses are complying less than their larger counterparts.

Regardless of whether you're acting on behalf of employers or you are responsible for automatic enrolment within your business being a member of the 'non compliant' club is not a club you want to join.

"Why?" I hear you ask. Let me tell you about the impact of automatic enrolment...

Chapter 2

The impact of Automatic Enrolment

So we've talked about the background behind automatic enrolment and the 'three circles' employers need to comply with.

However now it's time to start talking practically by initially trying to provide you with the answer to one question…

How does automatic enrolment impact you?

Now the answer to this question obviously depends on who you are!

The simple answer is if you employ, or work in a business where your job involves either complying with legislation, payroll, pensions or HR (and in many smaller businesses these roles are fulfilled by the same person) auto enrolment will impact you.

If you're an accountant, payroll bureaux, financial adviser or any other professional who has employer clients it's likely that auto enrolment will impact you too.

If you work for a pension provider or payroll software company it's absolutely certain you'll feel the impact of auto enrolment if you haven't done so already.

If you're an employee and don't fit into one of the categories above auto enrolment will definitely impact you too although probably not directly and in depth enough for you to need to read this book (unless you're responsible for managing automatic enrolment within your business).

I'd suggest you read something else. How about a nice Sherlock Holmes?

However for employers and the professionals who work with them please do read on…

First let's explore how automatic enrolment impacts employers….

So, How does auto enrolment impact employers?

Auto Enrolment impacts employers in a number of different ways.

First let's explore the implications for employers and as a starting point let's talk money…

As part of auto enrolment law employers may need to make contributions into a pension scheme for many of their employees.

I use the word 'may' intentionally as whether employers need to make contributions for their teams depend on a number of factors we'll explore later in this book.

We'll also explore the contribution levels so you can work out the actual cost to your business later on in this book however at this stage it's important to be aware of the fact that an unavoidable part of auto enrolment regulation is the fact that most employers need to make contributions.

In addition to the cost of any pension contributions there's also the cost of any systems you need to update or purchase to support you with your automatic enrolment obligations.

These may include support solutions like www.aeinabox.co.uk, upgrades to your existing payroll solution or 'middleware' (the software designed to help you perform certain functions of auto enrolment if you're payroll isn't up to the job)

It's important when looking at how automatic enrolment impacts your business you take into account not only pension contributions but also what you might need to pay for upgrading your existing payroll software or additional external support.

Considering the level of fines potentially imposed when employers get automatic enrolment wrong there are certain more established SME businesses who are happy to pay us and firms like us to solve the automatic enrolment challenge.

Also as more firms comply with automatic enrolment successfully the reality is that if you're in an industry or profession where finding the right people for your business is increasingly tough it's worth consulting with an employee benefits consultant to ensure that you've got a range of benefits which help attract, reward and retain the right people.

So whilst the support you can get to help you with your automatic enrolment obligations are significantly reducing in cost the reality is that there still is a cost associated with getting the right help for you and your business.

However, whilst employers often underestimate the costs of getting the right support the reality is that most employers underestimated one thing over any other.

The 'time cost' of complying with automatic enrolment.

The time either you or the people within your business need to spend on auto enrolment depends on a number of factors.

These will include your current systems, the complexity and nature of your business as well as whether you've got some of the components of auto enrolment already in place (like for example an existing pension scheme which already complies with the regulation).

We'll talk about the time you need to prepare for auto enrolment in your particular business later in the book however in our experience there's a universal rule which applies to all businesses....

The earlier you start to prepare and plan for auto enrolment the smoother the process will be.

Now all of this seems like a decent amount of work and will be a financial cost for employers to undertake on top of running their businesses. To be perfectly frank it is.

However with every cloud there's a silver lining.

Managed and communicated the right way automatic enrolment can be a force for good.

If managed in the right way automatic enrolment will be a powerful tool to engage your workforce, recruit and retain the best people and show that you're committed not only to your teams short term financial needs but are actively involved in helping them plan for their financial future.

Many larger businesses used auto enrolment as an opportunity to educate and empower employees to save for their financial future.

This meant that large employers took a potentially painful piece of regulation and used it as an opportunity to develop a more loyal and more engaged workforce.

It's interesting to see that although employees have the right to opt out (more on this later) and many commentators assumed the opt out rates were going to be significant, especially for lower paid employees, the reality is that most employees decide to continue to contribute to a pension scheme.

This trend of relatively low opt out rates has in our experience continued within smaller businesses with low opt out rates even in the smallest of businesses.

This could be for a number of reasons. However the optimist in me feels that if you give most of us the opportunity to save for our financial futures and make the process as easy as possible they'll save and therefore the number of opt outs will remain relatively low.

Now, typically with large employers we worked with them over a 12 to 18 month period. However we've found that for smaller businesses a period of 6 to 9 months prior to their staging date is plenty of time for smaller businesses to prepare, plan and complete the tasks they need to in order to fully comply with the new rules.

For many small businesses 6 to 9 months to plan for auto enrolment might seem like a long time.

However the fact that auto enrolment will impact many areas of your business, including how you manage your payroll, communicate with your employees and potentially need to change your employment contracts means that the longer you have to prepare the more likely you are to comply effectively.
It's also important to bear in mind that whilst planning for auto enrolment isn't a full time job it is an additional set of tasks you need to manage either within your business or on top of the 'day job'.

This means preparing earlier provides you with a bit more time to spread out many of the tasks you need to complete in order to ensure they're done with minimum disruption to the day to day running of your business.

We've found that the last thing most businesses want is a rush to comply.

This creates short term but relatively major disruption instead of a slightly longer plan but with a smoother journey along the way.

This smoother journey to auto enrolment compliance in our experience leads to a less disruptive and more successful journey for the employers who take this approach.

So, auto enrolment regulation comes with a time cost and a financial cost. However there's one additional cost which will impact employers when complying with auto enrolment. The cost of change.

The process of complying with auto enrolment might not only take time and money. It also might mean that you've got to change some of the processes within your business.

For example many of the employers we've worked with have had to change the their employment contracts, have decided to change the payroll and business management software they use or decide to use payroll software when they haven't previously.

In addition to this other employers have changed the professionals they use to help them manage certain aspects of their business (for example if you're using a payroll bureau who can't cope with auto enrolment or using a financial adviser with little understanding of the auto enrolment market).

These changes mean employers and the professionals they work with have to make additional decisions.

There are a number of questions which employers need to consider…

For example…

Do we keep the software we've got to make our lives easier or use a new system with more auto enrolment functionality?

Do we bring in an auto enrolment specialists or use a system designed to help us meet our regulatory responsibilities?

How do we decide who's best within our business to manage auto enrolment and ensure that our business is compliant?

These additional decisions, as well as any additional changes businesses make based on these changes, will take time and effort within their business.

As you can see the auto enrolment obligations an employer has are wide ranging and comes with not only financial costs but also time costs and the effort it takes employers to change some of their systems and processes within their own businesses.

For many of these employers they might get external help, either from their accountants, payroll bureaus or financial advisers.

Therefore regardless of whether you're an professional who helps employers, or an employer who is looking for help from these professionals it's worth taking some time explore some of the challenges professionals face when attempting to help employers. Now the scope and depth of the new rules mean that many employers are considering the impact of automatic enrolment and thinking about whether they can ignore complying with the regulation…

So, let's answer that next.

Can employers ignore automatic enrolment?

One of the questions I get asked quite a lot is…

"As a business owner and employer can I choose not to comply with this new company pension legislation?"

There's an easy answer to this…

You can…but you really shouldn't.

The responsibility for complying with automatic enrolment legislation is clear.

The responsibility for complying with automatic enrolment sits firmly with the employer.

If employers don't comply with the regulation there are significant penalties for not doing what you need to.

The first step the regulator will take if you don't comply is they'll issue a fixed penalty notice.

This charge is £400 and is a one off however it's only the start of the fines which are levied for not complying with the rules.

Next comes the daily penalties which for smaller businesses range from £50 for businesses who employ up to 4 individuals to up to £500 per day for business who employ between 4 and 50 employees.

This 'daily fine' can be charged each and every day including Saturdays, Sundays, Bank Holidays and Christmas day (as well as your birthday!)

Number of employees	Prescribed Daily Rate
1 - 4	£50
5 – 49	£500
50 – 249	£2,500
250 – 499	£5,000
500 or more	£10,000

In addition to this, if you don't pay the contributions into your pension scheme in an appropriate manner there are additional penalties and these fines can be up to £5,000 for individuals and up to £50,000 for organisations.

Also (yep, I've not finished yet!) there are the penalties for when you breach certain elements of the regulation, like for example encouraging the employees within your business to opt out of the pension scheme, there are additional fines which range from £1,000 all the way to £5,000.

To chase these fines The Pensions Regulator has a number of powers.

Firstly the regulator can take civil action. In addition to this they can prosecute employers who 'deliberately and wilfully fail to comply' and have if you're prosecuted for non-compliance the right to confiscate goods and restrain assets during a criminal investigation.

Therefore the message is clear. You can choose not to comply. But the size, frequency and severity of the penalties for non-compliance mean one thing....

It's far cheaper to comply with automatic enrolment legislation than it is to choose not to.

In addition to the financial penalties there are a few other areas you need to consider if you're an employer not intending to comply.

Firstly, when automatic enrolment is fully implemented all employers in the UK will have a workplace pension scheme in place and will be making contributions on behalf of their employees.

One of the big ideas behind automatic enrolment is that workplace pension savings will eventually be a common standard across all employers.

If you choose not to comply, in addition to the significant fines, it might be tough to compete for the most appropriate individuals to join your businesses team as well as retain your existing employees. Also, it's worth considering the potential impact on your businesses reputation.

If you run a business you understand that reputation has a significant impact on the success on your business.

Now your clients might not care whether they comply with these new rules. Alternatively they might assume that not complying with the rules is indicative of a business which ignores important issues.

So the significant fines, the escalation of these fines daily, the potential reputation risk on your business, the impact non-compliance could have on retention and recruitment and the fact that non-compliance can result in both civil action and prosecution all points in one direction…

Whilst complying with automatic enrolment takes significant effort, a decent amount of time and a change in a few of your business processes. Not complying with automatic enrolment

will more than likely be a lot worse.

How automatic enrolment impacts professionals?

Automatic enrolment not only impacts employers but also professionals, therefore I wanted to spend a little bit of page space talking about how automatic enrolment impacts the professionals who work to help businesses comply.

Before we start it's important to remember that many professionals who help employers are used to adapting to change on a regular basis already.

For accountants this has meant adapting the constant change of tax rules as well as having to change many of their internal systems and processes to ensure they comply with how some information is reported to the HMRC in 'real time' (the changes are appropriately titled 'real time information')

For payroll bureaus changes in the software market have had a decent impact and have meant many payroll bureaus have looked at their internal processes to see if their choice of payroll software means their businesses are as efficient as they could be.

For financial planners and advisers the landscape has changed incredibly in the past few years.

Changes in regulation changing the way financial advisers are paid has had an impact as well as changes in pension rules which have meant that they had to ensure their knowledge was regularly kept up to date.

Also constant changes in tax rules had a similar impact as accountants when it came to adapting both financial advisers business models as well as increasing the pressure on them to ensure that their knowledge remained up to date.

However although professionals are used to constant and consistent change, helping employers with automatic enrolment compliance for these professionals represents a unique challenge.

Many of the challenges professionals face, whilst often challenging, usually sit firmly in their scope of knowledge and expertise.

Most accountants (and payroll bureaus) managed to adapt to the 'real time information' challenges relatively easily as they understood the systems and processes within their businesses and what needed to be done to manage the change.

Most Payroll bureaus understand what software programs might be appropriate both for changing times and to ensure their particular business runs well.

and

The majority of financial advisers and planners understand the pensions world well, and have adapted to change both in their business models, systems and how they look after their clients appropriately.

However auto enrolment for all professionals, based on our experience and what the accountants, payroll bureaus and financial advisers tell us means that they are facing a unique challenge within their businesses.

You see auto enrolment is relatively unique. It's uniqueness comes from the fact that an employer's obligations don't naturally 'sit' in the realm of the accountant, the payroll bureau, or the financial adviser.

They sit within all three.

Traditionally accountants are great at business management usually including helping businesses put the systems and processes in place designed to help them comply with regulation but may not have the expertise in managing payroll.

Traditionally payroll bureaus know and manage payroll (which is a fundamental and intrinsic part of the auto enrolment process)

and

Traditionally financial advisers are great at putting in place and administering the pensions required as part of the auto enrolment process.

Therefore professionals who help employers with auto enrolment need to be multi-disciplinary, or have access to fellow professionals who fill the gap.

For businesses who provide accountancy services as well as managing payroll (and often also have financial advisory element to their businesses) this is less of an issue as employers can be helped and managed 'in house' by the various arms of the business.

However the challenge for these businesses is ensuring the constituent 'arms' of the business work together effectively to ensure that employers are looked after.

For accountancy, payroll and financial planning business without all of the constituent parts of the process 'in house' collaboration makes sense and we've seen many payroll bureaus and accountants team up with financial advisers to help their employers manage the auto enrolment process.

To fill many of the gaps in the marketplace we've seen a few alternatives emerge ranging from bespoke auto enrolment consultancy businesses to software providers designed to help the market.

For many professionals who want to help employers comply with auto enrolment the key challenges they face are clear…

The first challenge professionals face is having to fill gaps within their own businesses.

If you're a financial adviser who works in the auto enrolment space do you partner up with an accountant and/or payroll bureau to fill some of the gaps in your proposition?

If you're an accountant do you partner with payroll (if you don't already provide this service) and a financial adviser to fill the gap?

If you run a payroll business do you partner with a financial adviser and an accountant to fill the gap?

However the second challenge professionals who help employers with auto enrolment face is potentially the greater one and is approaching fast.

With hundreds of thousands of employers approaching their 'staging date', really soon there's a decent risk that demand from employers who need your help with auto enrolment will exceed supply.

Also, it's likely that if you're an accountant or payroll bureau you've potentially got a decent number of employers 'on your books' as existing clients who need (and expect) your help managing the process of auto enrolment.

This means that, if you're a professional who's dealing with auto enrolment within their business, the systems and processes within your businesses need to be streamlined to ensure you have the ability to potentially help the huge influx of employers who need to meet the rules.

We're seeing professionals mange this capacity in a couple of ways.

There are the professionals who are introducing their own auto enrolment processes.

These processes include payroll but also include provisions to help with both the pension and regulation element employers need to comply with (and therefore professionals who manage auto enrolment internally aren't usually solely reliant on their payroll software).

Alternatively we're also seeing professionals use software solutions to manage their clients auto enrolment needs.

In an ideal world there would be one piece of software which managed the auto enrolment tasks within payroll, deals with the pensions recommendation together with ensuring employers met all of their regulatory responsibilities.

However as I write this the reality is that there isn't one piece of software which does all of these jobs.

So usually, professionals who use software in this marketplace use more than one piece.

They use payroll software with auto enrolment functionality to manage the obligations under payroll and then an additional piece of software designed to meet both the pension selection and compliance measures.

I'm an employer – should I care?

Now if you're an employer reading this, it's unlikely you're not too interested in how professionals are managing in the changing auto enrolment marketplace.

The answer is you should especially if you've chosen to work with a professional to assist you in managing your automatic enrolment obligations as you need to be confident that they are able to do the job.

Understanding the challenges they face allows you to ask the right questions in order to understand whether they're best equipped to do the job.

However it's also important to consider other factors if you've chosen to work with a professional.

Working with a professional to help you comply with automatic enrolment

Whilst many employers will opt to use software tools (or take a completely DIY approach) to comply with auto enrolment regulation there are plenty of employers who will choose to work with a professional to help guide them through the process.

However for many employers we speak to, and who are considering the financial, commercial and reputation related implications of getting this regulation wrong, choosing the right professional to work with can be a difficult decision.

However this chapter is to ensure that if you are an employer who is looking for external professional support this difficult decision on who to choose is made far easier.

Firstly we're going to go through the different type of professional help available in the market from accountants and payroll bureaus through to financial advisers, specialist auto enrolment service providers and software services.

Then we're going to talk about some of the factors you should consider when choosing a professional to work with to help you with the auto enrolment process as well as highlighting some of the questions you should ask of the professionals you might want to work with to help you make the most appropriate decision.

However before we do this let's talk about why as an employer you might consider working with a professional (as opposed to taking a 'do it yourself' approach) and the importance of shopping around.

Why using a professional might be right to help you through the auto enrolment process

If you're a small business employer one of the first considerations, and one which might put you off seeking professional advice to help you is cost.

In terms of cold hard cash working with a professional can be a more expensive route to take for your business than dealing with the obligations internally.

It's natural to consider the financial implications of 'getting a man/woman in' or using a software solution to help do the job.

However the important thing to do is to compare this with the implications of not getting external help and to illustrate this I want to make a confession.

Whilst I'm pretty good at helping employers meet their auto enrolment obligations, I'm absolutely rubbish at DIY!

Now you may be asking yourself why this is relevant. Why should you care how good I am at putting together furniture, or painting, or fitting carpet?

The answer is you shouldn't.

However when I've got a job to do round the house I've got a choice.

I can either go through the frustration of sitting on my living room floor for a few hours surrounded by bits of wood, metal and bolts as well as spending just as long trying to make sense of the instructions and trying to work out whether the widget in my hand is 'bolt a' or 'attachment c' or I can get someone in who has the skills and ability to build the bookcase in a quarter of the time and half the effort.

So now, every time I've got a practical job to do in the house (and especially as I'm as impractical when it comes to DIY as I am) I've got to make a choice.

Do I spend the time to do the job, or is it more time efficient to get someone in to do the job?

Most small businesses are great at what they do.

Whether you're a plumber, a restaurateur, shopkeeper or doing something completely different most small businesses want to spend their time focusing on what they need to do to make their businesses continue to grow and thrive.

Also, most small businesses are good at what they do because they know their profession really well. They do it every day. They've learnt more and slowly and gradually continue to improve at their particular business, profession or trade.

So, for many small businesses (including maybe yours) working with an auto enrolment specialist or alternatively using software can make more sense than taking a 'DIY' approach.

This is because working with a professional or using a support service will give you access to both systems and expertise and therefore should make your journey to automatic enrolment compliance smoother.

This is because it'll allows both you and your business to focus on what you do best….

Spending time focussing on what you're good at.

It's likely that true professionals who offer an auto enrolment compliance service will be doing this sort of work day in day out, keeping up with the changes both in regulation and the marketplace as well as having the ability to guide you through the process you need to follow at every step of the way, reminding you of deadlines where appropriate and taking on specific tasks for you if appropriate.

For these auto enrolment professionals helping employers regularly also ensures that their skill set in supporting businesses with their auto enrolment obligations continues to grow.

Continuously helping employers with their obligations also ensures that professionals gradually make their processes more efficient and allows them to complete the tasks required to comply with auto enrolment in a far shorter time period then if you were 'doing it yourself' (as well as ensuring you can focus on your business).

Now for many employers the decision to engage a professional to help you (or use software to support you) with your auto enrolment obligations might not be the right route to take.

Ultimately, the decision to take a 'DIY' approach or to 'get a man in' to help you ensure you can comply with auto enrolment will be up to you.

However if you've decided to use an auto enrolment professional to help you through complying with the regulation there's an additional question you need to ask.

How do I pick a professional or support service to help me?

Over the last few years we've helped a decent number of employers with their auto enrolment obligations.

We've also spent a decent amount of time with other respected professionals learning what they do to help their clients through the auto enrolment process as well as seeing and hearing about 'bad practice' where so called 'professionals' haven't done a particularly good job as well as developing AE in a Box, which as I've mentioned helps empower employers to perform the tasks themselves.

In our experience there are seven factors you as an employer should consider when making the decision to work with a professional to help you meet your auto enrolment obligations.

If you're considering using a technological based support solution the questions you might want to ask will be slightly different.

So, in addition to the questions you might want to ask a professional, I've also included some questions to ask a software provider if you've decided to go down this route.

So, Let's explore the factors you need to consider...

1. Practical experience

When you're selecting any professional you're working with, from your accountant, lawyer or electrician you want to be sure that the particular professional has sufficient practical experience helping people like you.

Engaging an automatic enrolment enrolment professional to help you comply is no different.

So feel free to ask some questions. Ask them to tell you about how they've practically helped previous clients and whether they've helped similar companies in your particular business sector (this could come in handy, especially if you work in temporary recruitment or retail).

Questions which might be worth asking are….

Have you helped businesses like mine comply with auto enrolment?

What have your learned about auto enrolment through working practically with employers?

Tell me about the different type of businesses you've helped comply with auto enrolment?

If you've decided to use a software package it's important to understand who's behind the software but in addition to this it's important to understand whether feedback has been received and acted upon

Have they tested their software with particular employers and made improvements to the software based on the feedback?

How many employers have used the software already?

How many continue to use it?

So, we've established that practical experience is useful but this experience needs to go hand in hand with number two on our list…

2. *Technical Knowledge*

Whilst practical knowledge is valuable you also want to work with someone who knows their beans technically.

The easiest way to explore how technically capable the particular professional you're looking to engage is to ask them about their qualifications specifically around the auto enrolment market.

As I write this there's only one particular qualification related specifically to auto enrolment.

This is run by the PMI (the Pensions Management Institute) and is called 'the certificate in Pensions Automatic Enrolment'.

It's therefore worth checking that the particular professional you're considering working with has taken this exam, or if not whether they intend to.

Choosing someone who has already passed this exam means that you're selecting a professional who has the specific knowledge around helping you meet your automatic enrolment challenge and has a commitment to professional development.

In addition to the professionals qualification it's worth checking how long and how often the auto enrolment professional your considering working with has spent learning about auto enrolment and well as how long they've spent actively engaged in the auto enrolment market.

To check you're comfortable with the standard of technical knowledge the professional you're considering has the questions you might want to consider asking are….

Do you hold the Pensions Management Institute Auto Enrolment qualification?

How do you keep up do date with regulation when it changes?

How do you keep up to date with changes in the marketplace?

How much time do you spend practically working with employers?

If you're using auto enrolment software it's worth asking who's been involved with building and developing the technical elements of the software and they're particular level of technical knowledge by asking the similar questions above.

3. Project Management Skill and experience

As you'll read a little later in this book, for most employers the process of complying with auto enrolment involves a project.

This project will be designed to get them from not complying to being an employer who's met their regulatory responsibilities.

This project, if done well, will start months before their staging date and continue indefinitely.

Therefore it's important to understand, if you've decided to work with a professional, how experienced they are in creating a project plan, delivering the project on time and on target.

Many auto enrolment professionals are pretty adept at managing projects and implementing solutions that work.

However it's worth double checking their level of project management experience by asking some questions around their systems and processes. Questions like…

Tell me about the processes you follow to help employers comply?

What systems do you use to manage your workload?

How do we manage what you do as part of this project and what we (as an employer) do?

What's the typical work flow for one of your projects and what are the typical timescales?

If you're using software it's important to understand how it helps you, as an employer, manage your auto enrolment project.

Therefore it's worth checking with the software provider how the process of using the software works and applying some of the questions above to the software in question.

4. What their current and previous clients say

If you're engaging in any professional service it's important to ask for testimonials to help you understand how previous clients have found the experience.

The questions to ask in this regard are clear:-

Can you show me some testimonials for users of your service?

Can I speak to some existing clients who use your service who can tell me about their experience working with you?

5. Someone who always works in your best interest.

When considering working with a professional or software service it's worth asking some questions about how they will work in your best interest

You want the professional you work with, or the software service you've decided to use to guide you in the right direction at every step of the way with the minimum of fuss but also provides a solution that works for you.

This means not only thinking about the most appropriate pension and software solution from the marketplace (instead of just providing one pension choice) but also considering what you may have within your business already and whether this is appropriate.

For example, if you've got a pension or payroll software already in place within your business will this meet your obligations under auto enrolment.

After all, using what you've got in place might be a better approach than setting up new pension provisions and software solutions.

That's why if you decide to work with a professional you need to choose one who is providing a solution which makes complying with automatic enrolment as straightforward as possible by working in your best interest and using your existing pension and payroll software provider if they do the job.

6. Commitment to providing you with an ongoing service

There's a common misconception that the obligations under auto enrolment obligation stop when an employer has completed all the tasks up to their staging date.

However in reality the obligations an employer has to manage when it comes to auto enrolment starts before their staging date but never ends.

Automatic enrolment regulation does change and the odds are it will continue to change over time for a couple of reasons we'll talk about later.

Therefore if you're either working with a professional or alternatively a software service one of the most pertinent questions you need to ask is…

How will working with you not only ensure that my business complies with auto enrolment now but also in the future?

It's also important to consider how the professional you work with charges.

For example if you pay "one off" for a service it's worth asking how that particular professional (or software package) can afford to ensure you're up to date with changing regulation indefinitely when the rules change?

It's also worth asking if the service they're providing is intended to just ensure you comply up to your staging date or provides you with an ongoing service.

7. Value

The costs of getting auto enrolment wrong are significant. Therefore I'd always suggest if you're looking to engage with a professional focus on engaging a service which you're confident will do a proper job on your behalf

However there's no denying that if you've chosen to work with a professional or intend to use software to support you with ensuring you meet auto enrolment regulation one factor you need to absolutely consider is cost.

Saying that it's worth remembering the old saying…

Price is what you pay. Value is what you get.

Instead of focusing purely on cost it's worth looking instead at value.

For instance the questions you might want to ask might be…

If I work with you how much time will this potentially save me?

How much work will I need to do? How much work will you take on?

How much time will my element of the project take to do?

Can you give me an example of how you've saved an employer both time and money by working with you?

The cost of engaging with an automatic enrolment professional depends on a number of factors and the market seems to consistently change and develop.

Therefore when it comes to working with a professional (if you've decided to do this) it makes sense to consider two or three options and making a decision based on both cost, value and the other factors we've described in this chapter.

One important point about value is that there are certain auto enrolment compliance propositions who purport to be 'free' for employers.

It's important to note that whilst these propositions may be 'free' for employers to use there is a cost.

This cost is usually tied up with the pension they put in place on your behalf and is therefore paid as a cost to your employees.

Personally I'm not too keen on this approach. Whilst this might save employers money in costs it's important to consider the longer term impact on your business of using these propositions.

For example, let's assume you use one of these 'free' propositions (which your employees actually pay for) and in future years your workforce come to the understanding that they've been paying for a service which helps you (as an employer) meets your obligations? What impact will that have on the morale of your staff?

Therefore whilst these 'free' propositions are initially pretty attractive (we all like 'free' stuff don't we) it's important to consider the longer term implications of selecting one of these auto enrolment solutions over and above a paid one.

Working with a professional or using a software service is a personal choice. It'll be right for many employers but not right for others.

However regardless of whether an employer decides to use software, work with a professional or decides to entirely "Do it Themselves" there is one thing which will drastically increase the chances of employers complying well and avoiding the penalties for not doing so.

Having a decent automatic enrolment plan.

Chapter 3

Creating your automatic enrolment plan

In the first edition of this book this chapter started by explaining that the key factor to ensure that you comply successfully is time.

Now since the last edition the time it should take to comply with automatic enrolment fully should have reduced considerabl.

However it's important to consider that for some small and medium sized employers taking the time to ensure you comply with automatic enrolment successfully it seems to be a less important factor than previously due to the efficient of many of the pensions and payroll platforms currently available.7

However let's be clear it's still important to start to plan to ensure you can comply with automatic enrolment if your business is within 9 months of it's staging date.

Now you also might be thinking that you won't need 9 months to prepare your business for this change in regulation.

The reality is you might not. However there are good reasons why we recommend you start to prepare 9 months prior to your staging date. Let me explain why.

When you're in the months prior to your staging date you need to complete a bunch of tasks in order to prepare properly.

These tasks if complete smoothly might mean you could potentially complete them all with time to spare even if you don't prepare early.

However as in life, automatic enrolment compliance doesn't always run particularly smoothly.

Let's assume for example you start to prepare, because you think it's plenty of time, 3 months prior to your staging date.

Firstly you want to understand enough about auto enrolment to comply successfully.

This might be by reading the guidance from the pensions regulator, it might be by reading this book, it might be through engaging with a professional, it might be by using a support solution like AE in a Box or it might be a combination of these things.

Let's assume you've then got to decide on the most appropriate approach for your business.
It's an important decision so you take a couple of weeks to understand more about your obligations and decide on the best approach for your business.

Let's then assume that you've decided to comply with auto enrolment yourself without any support (apart from understanding enough about the regulation to comply) and you've tasked someone within your business to understand enough about auto enrolment to manage this internally.

Let's also assume that the person you task to do this (on top of the other tasks they need to perform within your business) takes another couple of weeks to fully understand your obligations as an employer.

After that the person who you've tasked to manage auto enrolment within your business checks whether your existing pension provider can be used as your auto enrolment scheme and after waiting 2 weeks for a definitive response from them you find they don't.

The person who's dealing with auto enrolment doesn't have a chance to apply for a new pension for another couple of weeks (because naturally you're doing what's important which is running your business) you then apply for a auto enrolment pension scheme.

Then disaster strikes! The individual tasked with auto enrolment checks your payroll software and find it doesn't do what you need to do to help you comply with auto enrolment.

You decide that you want to use an alternative payroll software and start to shop around for alternative payroll software providers.

This isn't a decision you want to rush into as you want to make sure the payroll software you decide to switch to is fit for purpose so you take another few weeks (let's say three weeks) to decide.

You then decide what software you want to use and then need to migrate all of your information over from your old payroll provider to your new one. This, at best, might take another couple of weeks.

You then realise you need to make some changes to your employment contracts due to auto enrolment legislation and need to research into the changes you need to make as well as making the appropriate changes. Let's assume this take another couple of weeks.

Now I know I've painted a worst case scenario and we've made a bunch of assumptions to get to this figure but all or any of these things can and have occurred with employers who have had to prepare for the auto enrolment process.
So, if we assume that occurs we're now 15 weeks into the auto enrolment project. If an employer who has left 12 weeks (3

months) prior to their staging date it's obvious that they haven't got enough time to comply successfully without rushing certain elements of the process.

Also for the purposes of this example we've ignored many of the other tasks employers need to complete prior to staging date and we haven't taken into account the fact that the person who is dealing with auto enrolment within your business might have holiday, or be off sick, or leave the business (meaning which you might need to pick up a project yourself or assign someone else within your business to do the job).

We've also for the purposes of this example not taken into account the time you need to spend communicating with the team within your business or spending any time to select a new pension.

So, whilst 9 months might seem like a long time and whilst you (if you're an employer) or your clients (as a professional) might not need all of this time to comply it makes sense to ensure that you start to prepare sooner rather than later.

The reason we recommend employers comply 9 months prior to their staging date is purely due to the fact that in our experience this period allows employers plenty of time to make important decisions, plenty of time to negotiate any 'bumps in the road' and plenty of time to ensure the job of initially complying with auto enrolment regulation is done well.

If you're a professional who has clients with less than 9 months to comply or an employer who has less than 9 months to comply don't panic. However take action now....

And with that in mind let's talk about the first step towards successful auto enrolment compliance....

Creating your auto enrolment plan.

How to start planning for automatic enrolment

In this section we're going to talk about the first step towards successful auto enrolment compliance for any business..

Putting a plan in place.

Now people tend to plan in a bunch of different ways.

Some people like lengthy documents detailing all parts and all potential variables of a particular plan. Some people like rough and ready one page versions covering the headline points of the plan and then working on the detail as they go through.

Some people use a word document, others like to plan using mind maps tools. Others simply plan with a pen and paper.

However most successful plans have one thing in common…

They start with the end in mind.

When it comes to employers, regardless of the size, scale and scope of their business, who need to comply with auto enrolment the 'end' is always the same.

Employers need to successfully comply with current auto enrolment regulation by their staging date and have a system in place to ensure they continue to comply as their obligations (and the rules) change.

In reality 'the end' of the plan for employers isn't really the end.

Automatic enrolment regulation will continue to impact businesses not only now but also long into the future (more on this later).

However the first step you (if you're an employer) or your clients (if you're a professional helping employers with auto enrolment) need to make is to ensure a specific number of tasks are completed by a fixed point in time (the employers staging date).

To start with the 'end in mind' when it comes to an auto enrolment project there's a few pieces of information you need to get. Firstly you need to know you're staging date. Now it's likely you've already received a letter from the regulator confirming this.

However if you haven't received (or have misplaced) this letter luckily discovering your staging date is relatively easy and you didn't check your staging date when I mentioned it earlier in this book take some time to do this now.

All you need to do this is have your PAYE reference number to hand then visit The Pension Regulators website[6]

Once you're on this page complete the form and you'll be able to find out what you're staging date is.

Once you know you're deadline you'll know how much time you've got to comply with the regulation.

If you've got more than 9 months until you're staging date, breathe easy (you've got a bit of time to comply).

Saying that it's worth having some form of system in place to ensure you're reminded closer to the time that you need to start implementing auto enrolment within your business.

You can do this in a number of ways, either by using the existing reminder systems within your business, having a date in the diary or by using a bespoke auto enrolment system which reminds you

---

[6] To find out your staging date go to
http://www.thepensionsregulator.gov.uk/employers/staging-date.aspx

when you're staging date is 9 months away like, for instance, AE in a Box.

If you've got 9 months or less until you're staging date let me make a humble suggestion…

Write your auto enrolment plan and start taking action today. Then start completing the tasks you need to do to ensure you're ready in plenty of time.

Once you've got your staging date you'll need to define what 'success' looks like.

Effectively the end result we want is to ensure your business **'complies with auto enrolment successfully'** and ensuring **'you've got the systems in place to ensure you continue to comply in the future'**.

What do you need to do next?

In this chapter I want to give you a framework for producing your automatic enrolment compliance plan.

However before I do that, let me treat you to a little disclaimer..

Whilst I'm going to make every effort to do so there's no way I can guarantee I'll cover everything you need to do to comply with auto enrolment within this book.

Also I'm not sure, dear reader, when you're reading this so regulation may have changed and the edition of the book you're reading might not be completely up to date.

The reason you're reading the 2nd edition of this book is because things changed in the year and a bit since we released the first edition.

Therefore I can't guarantee that by the time you read this edition other changes might not have occurred…

The purpose of this book is to ensure you're aware of the things you need to do within your businesses, give you some practical guidance but it's also designed to be easy to digest.

What this book isn't, although we've tried to make this as thorough as possible, isn't the absolutely most definitive guide to auto enrolment.

If you're looking for the most up to date, comprehensive and definitive guidance you could either check the pension regulators website or consider using a support solution like AE in a Box.

The pension regulators 'detailed guidance' and additional support

As I've mentioned the most definitive and thorough guide on how to comply with the automatic enrolment rules can be found within the detailed guidance[7]

As I write this, the detailed guidance provides links to the 14 in depth chapters and 14 appendices covering all of the specifics of automatic enrolment regulation.

Including appendices there are around 540 pages jam packed full of detailed guidance on the pension regulator website which although jam packed full of useful guidance might be a bit difficult to both take in and navigate through.

---

[7] The detailed guidance can be found at
http://www.thepensionsregulator.gov.uk/doc-library/automatic-enrolment-detailed-guidance.aspx

However if you're looking to dig deep into the regulation to find something specific because you need to confirm whether it applies to your business help is at hand.

I've found the easiest way to confirm and check where the regulation sits on specific points is to use the pension regulators helpline (you can find this number in the 'contact us' tab of the pension regulators website) or searching the website for the most relevant answer.

However for businesses who are concerned about highlighting to the regulator that they may have made mistakes within their business it's also worth looking at AE in a Box's 'ask the regulator' service which allows employers to ask the regulator specific questions anonymously.

Auto Enrolment regulation has changed since inception, can change at any time and is likely to change in the future as the rules become firmly established and then develop.

Therefore whilst this book should be massively useful in highlighting many of the things you need to consider, and despite the fact that we'll try and release up to date editions which reflect any changes this book won't be the best way to track these changes.

We'll talk about how auto enrolment, has, can and is likely to change in the future (and more importantly what you can do to efficiently stay ahead of the game) in a decent amount of detail later in this book.

So now we're done with our little disclaimer let's start helping you build your automatic enrolment plan. However let's start with the reason why it makes sense to have one...

"I don't need a plan....do I?"

Now I know at this stage, if you're like many smaller businesses we've spoken to about automatic enrolment, what you might be thinking.

"I don't need a specific plan to make changes in my business required under the new legislation…"

This might be true and as long as you comply with all of your regulatory responsibilities you're not going to be dragged over the coals for not having a specific plan.

Also, for many small businesses who are busy running their business and engaged in the 'day job' (doing the work your clients or customers pay you for) feel that planning for automatic enrolment may initially seem like a distraction instead of a beneficial exercise.

However it's important not to underestimate the changes you'll need to make to your systems and processes in order to comply with the new legislation.

In our experience the employers who comply smoothly and with minimal issues have taken the time to plan how they are going to comply with this regulation instead of just jumping in to the tasks they need to complete.

Also, like any fundamental change in your business processes and procedures, ensuring you've got a **clear actionable written plan** in place provides a bunch of valuable benefits.

The benefits of having a plan to comply with automatic enrolment aren't dissimilar with having a business plan or a plan for your personal finances.

However, there's some value in reiterating the benefits of having a specific plan when it comes to complying with automatic enrolment regulation…

Having a written plan can help ensure you don't miss specific tasks.

Having a clear plan in place provides you with an opportunity to think with clarity about the specific tasks you need to complete, think about the timescale for these tasks and importantly act as a checklist for the tasks you've done and haven't done.

Therefore a written plan can act as a checklist for the tasks you need to complete. Although there are specific project management tools which can help you do this just as well or can work as an efficient way to track all the tasks you need to complete (In the interests of full disclosure it's important to mention that AE in a Box provides this functionality).

Having a written plan ensures you can outline clear actions and who's responsible.

Taking some time to think about how you're business is going to comply with automatic enrolment allows you to think and then clearly document who's responsible.

This allows you to either delegate 'tasks' to certain individuals within your business, do these tasks yourself or assign these tasks to an external consultant.

Also, having your written plan documented allows you to ensure that all parties involved remain accountable.

If in your written plan you've assigned a specific task (let's say registering with the regulator once you've complied) to a particular individual within your business your plan allows you to efficiently and effectively track.

Having a written plan helps you think about how to overcome specific challenges.

In our experience there are a number of points in the journey towards automatic enrolment compliance where you'll need to make some key decisions.

We'll continue to talk about the specific challenges you need to make throughout the book however in our experience making some initial decisions at the start of the process makes sense.

These include the decisions you'll need to make about dealing with postponement, contribution levels and communications (terms which may not mean a lot now but you'll fully understand when you've finished the book!)

Having made decisions on how to deal with specific issues in the planning stage of your automatic enrolment journey up front as opposed to when you face them will avoid delays when you're in a position where you should be taking action to comply

Building your automatic enrolment plan

I'm not a big fan of planning for planning sakes. After all shouldn't a plan be practical in nature detailing a list of clear actions so we can get stuff done?

Therefore when we talk about creating a document which is action focussed as opposed to just a navel gazing, 'planning for planning's sake' style document.

Also, your automatic enrolment plan also doesn't need to be a huge document detailing every intricacy of your plan.

Whilst it's important you and your business fully and thoroughly complies with its automatic enrolment obligations I'm keen we don't overkill the planning stage.

So, now we know that the most useful plan is a practical planning document which is relatively short in length I want to explain how this book will help you build a clear plan.

So next what we're going to do is detail what should be included in your automatic enrolment plan whilst pointing to other chapters which will go into more detail about the clear actions you need to take.

Secondly, and to give you an idea of what a practical automatic enrolment plan will look like you'll find a typical example in Appendix I of this book.

Whilst your automatic enrolment plan might look slightly (or even fundamentally) different this will give you an idea of what to consider.

So, without any further ado, let's talk about the headlines of your automatic enrolment plan together with a description of what should be included...

Part 1 - Staging date and timeline

As we're starting with 'the end in mind' your plan should start by highlighting when all of the preparatory tasks need to be completed by.

For example (and as you'll see in the example report in appendix i) an appropriate start to the plan (and assuming I've written this on the 1st of January 2017) might be:-

ABC Employers staging date is the 1st of August 2017. Therefore we have 6 months from today to comply

Part 2 – Responsibility and contingency

One of the important parts of your automatic enrolment plan is to decide who within the business is responsible for complying with automatic enrolment.

In our experience within larger businesses the responsibility for automatic enrolment tends to be spread over a number of people.

However in most smaller businesses the responsibility to ensure you comply usually sits on the shoulders of one individual or sometimes two.

Therefore it's important to decide who this is going to be.

However one important point when thinking about who's responsible is it's important to have a contingency plan.

There has been occasion that employers have failed to comply in the past due to the individual assigned the task of helping an employer comply has either been off sick for a lengthy period or has left the business.

Therefore it's worth thinking about both the individual you choose to manage your automatic enrolment project together with the implications if they couldn't finish this project.

There are two practical actions you can take to have a decent contingency plan in place...

Firstly, ensure you have assigned another individual within your business (I appreciate that in many small businesses this may be one of the owners) to take over if the initial project manager is unable to finish the job.

Secondly, it's important to have a clear record of the tasks completed and the tasks still outstanding so that you can quickly continue your journey through to automatic enrolment compliance.

To give you an example of how this might be achieved, users of AE in a Box have access to an audit trail showing not only the time and date of completed tasks but who completed each 'job'.

Regardless of whether or not you decide to use AE in a Box you should have a similar way to track the 'tasks' you complete along the way.
The reality with automatic enrolment is that you need to comply with the regulation within specific timescales.

Therefore thinking about who would manage the automatic enrolment project if the individual you've assigned the project to can't continue (due to sickness, or leaving the business, or any other reason) and putting a line or so in your plan to cover this contingency makes practical sense.

Part 3 – Understand automatic enrolment

Once you've assigned someone to manage the automatic enrolment project one of the first things you need to do is take some time to understand how automatic enrolment works within your business.

As you're reading this book you're already well on the way to doing this however it's also reviewing the detailed guidance on the pension regulators website to see the potential gaps in knowledge you need to fill.

However you may decide, or may have already decided, to get specific support to help you comply with either all or some of the aspects of the automatic enrolment process.

Making the decision to get further support will obviously impact how much you need to know.

If you decide that you just want help in a specific aspects of the automatic enrolment process (i.e. pension selection & ongoing compliance) this will change how much you need to know today and how much you can rely on the support you receive from alternative sources.

That's why the next part of your automatic enrolment plan should be...

Part 4 – Deciding on the specific support you need to help you comply (see chapters 2 & 7 in more detail)

In this part of the plan you should be looking more specifically at the support you want and need to help you comply with the regulation.

It's important to be crystal clear if you're either working with a professional or using a support service the specifics of the service they provide.

We've already explored some of the things you should look for when selecting a professional to work with in Chapter 2 and we'll go into more detail in Chapter 7.

However the key factor when selecting a professional or support service to use to help you with automatic enrolment is to understand what they'll do, and more importantly, won't do so you can fully comply.

It's also worth pointing out that if you decide to engage with a professional on a consultancy basis your automatic enrolment plan, if you're like the majority of our consultancy clients, will be done in conjunction with the professional you've chosen to work with.

Part 5 – Confirming, clarifying and recording the actions you need to take within the 'circle of regulation' (see chapter 4 for more detail)

Whilst automatic enrolment is about all of the "three circles" (payroll, pensions and regulation) with numerous tasks to complete in all three areas the one which underpins the entire process is the 'circle of regulation'.

Therefore a major part of your plan should be detailing the actions you need to take and the decisions you've made to comply in specific areas of the regulation.

You'll find explanations of the major areas you need to make decisions in, together with some guidance on what you need to consider whilst making these decisions fully detailed in chapter 4 as well as an example of how a business might plan using the example report in appendix i.

We'll talk about the specific decisions you need to make, and the information you need in order to make these decisions in the next chapter however this part of your plan should include detail on the following:-

- Whether you've decided to bring your staging date forward and the action you need to take in order to do this.
- Who within your business is going to be your nominated point of contact.
- Calculating who within your business needs to be enrolled.
- How you're going to review and whether you need to change your employment contracts.
- How you're going to raise awareness with your workforce about automatic enrolment.
- How you're going to calculate your contributions
- Whether you're going to use postponement and for how long.

- Your process for opting in individuals when requested
- Your process for individuals opting out
- How you're going to communicate with your team and who's responsible for this
- When you're going to register with the regulator and clarity on who's responsible for doing this.
- How you're going to be sure to increase contributions when you need to as part of the minimum contribution levels.
- How you intend to keep records for the minimum period of time the legislation dictates.
- How you intend to continue to keep up to date with changes in the regulation and comply on an ongoing basis with any tasks which need to be done.

Once you've included in your plan how you intend to deal with all these issues it's time to move onto the next stage of planning.

Part 6 – Confirming, clarifying and recording the actions you need to take within the 'circle of pensions' (see chapter 5 for more detail)

Similarly to the process you followed when looking at the 'circle of regulation' there's a number of issues you need to consider when thinking about the 'circle of pensions'.

Again we'll cover these off one by one and in a decent amount of detail in Chapter 5 but so you've got an overview the questions you'll need to think about, answer and then document in your plan are...

- Have you got an existing pension?
- Have you checked whether you can use this existing scheme to help you comply with your automatic enrolment obligations?

- If you haven't got an existing scheme you can use, are you going to seek professional advice to help you select a scheme, use a support service or make the decision yourself?
- If you're going to work with a professional specifically to help you select a new pension scheme how are you going to select the professional you work with?
- What factors are important to you, your business and your employees when selecting a pension scheme? (these should include the financial strength of the provider, cost, fund choice, compatibility with payroll and/or good levels of service)
- Who's going to be responsible for pension selection within your business? Are you going to talk to your employees about what they want in a scheme?
- Who's responsible for the pension application process either within your business? (it's important to note that the administration process might be managed

Once you've considered and decided on all of the aspects in relation to your pension requirements and then documented them in your plan it's time to move onto…

Part 7 - Confirming, clarifying and recording the actions you need to take with the 'circle of payroll' (see chapter 6 for more detail)

In this part of your plan you'll be thinking about and then confirming the action you need to take in relation to payroll.

Again we'll cover off the specifics in chapter 6 however in respect for this part of the automatic enrolment puzzle the questions you'll want to ask, answer and then document in your report are:-

- Who's going to be responsible for checking that your current payroll software or bureau is fit for purpose?

- Who's going to be responsible within your business for completing the specific payroll related tasks on a regular basis?
- Does your current payroll software (or bureau if you use one) provide the functionality required to ensure you comply with the regulation? This should include reference to whether your current payroll software or bureau provides the following functionality:-

  - Calculate who should be enrolled
  - Calculate pension contributions
  - Retain payroll related records as required by law
  - "Talk to" your pension provider of choice
  - Automatically enrol employees every three years
  - Issue mandatory communications

- If your current payroll software / bureau doesn't provide this functionality what plan have you got in place to 'fill the gaps'?
- Is it worth considering switching your payroll software / bureau to a service provider with better automatic enrolment functionality?
- Is it worth considering using 'middleware' to fill some of the gaps in auto enrolment functionality in your payroll or will this make your processes unnecessarily complex?
- How do your systems and processes take into account what your payroll software doesn't do to help you comply with the regulation?

Part 8 – Action timeline and taking action (see chapter 8)

Now you've explored and fully documented all of the required aspects of the automatic enrolment process the next step is to turn this into an action timeline.

This means taking all of the information you've gathered and the decisions you've made and to convert these into practical actions you need to take together with a clear timeline documenting when you want these actions to be completed.

You can find an example of an efficient way of laying out this timeline in the example planning document in appendix I.

It's important to note that the action timeline we've used in appendix I is just that....an example.

In the interests of brevity and to ensure you focus on the specific tasks applicable to your business this 'action timeline' isn't a full list of the tasks you need to complete.

It's important you consider your own timeline relative to your businesses staging date together with the specific tasks you need to complete in your plan as the "action timeline" shown in appendix I is only designed to provide a template of a useful format.

Also, and we'll talk about this in more depth in Chapter 7, it's important to remember that if you need help structuring an appropriate timeline to ensure you comply there are a bunch of commercial tools available.

These tools allow you to manage the automatic enrolment process efficiently with suggested timelines for each 'task' within the automatic enrolment process.

For example, AE in a Box provides this functionality as part of its support to employers and provides as part of its core functionality an automatic enrolment task management system and reminder service when specific tasks aren't completed within an appropriate timescale.

Part 9 – Complying on an ongoing basis (for more detail see chapter 9)

One of the most important things to remember about your obligations under the automatic enrolment regulation is when your businesses obligations cease under the new regulation…

The most straightforward answer? They don't.

One of the most important things to remember about automatic enrolment regulation is that business owners need to ensure that they continue to comply on a consistent ongoing basis.

It's a lot like other legislation which impacts employers, for example employment or tax law, in this regard.

Also it's important to remember the automatic enrolment regulation can (and does) change.

Some of these changes will apply to your business, some may not.

Some of the changes are established in the rules already (like the gradual increase in minimum contribution levels). Other changes haven't been established yet but will be confirmed as automatic enrolment legislation is refined over time.

We'll talk about this in more depth in Chapter 9 however suffice to say at this stage it's important to remember to have systems and processes in place to ensure your business continues to comply with the legislation in 2 main areas…

1) How to comply with upcoming changes you need to make within your business based on what's in the regulation today (for example – the gradual increase in minimum contribution levels you need to make within your business)

2) How to stay fully informed about the changes made in the regulation which means that you need to take action within your business.

So, now we've talked about what should be in your plan and provided you with a 'template' for your automatic enrolment plan the next step is to talk in more depth about the specific rules relating to automatic enrolment.

Therefore Ladies and Gentleman let's start the in depth journey by first exploring the first circle of automatic enrolment....

Regulation.

Chapter 4

Regulation
The first circle of Automatic Enrolment

In this chapter we'll talk about the first (and I'd argue the most important) circle of automatic enrolment.

The Regulation and how employers ensure they comply with it.

We'll explore step by step the important things you need to consider when complying with automatic enrolment regulation together with the practical action you need to take at every step of the way.

So, let's start at the start with one of the first things you need to do to comply with automatic enrolment regulation..

Confirming your Staging date

I've mentioned this already however I make no apologies for mentioning it again (it's really important!).

The first thing you want to do as part of your auto enrolment planning is to confirm your staging date.

Thankfully you can do this pretty easily.

All you need to do, as we've covered already, is visit the pensions regulator website with some information on your business (including your PAYE reference number) and you'll be able to find out when your business needs to be ready for auto enrolment.

However one thing we haven't covered already is that once you've got your staging date you'll need to make a decision.

Bringing your staging date forward

Once you know your staging date you've got a choice.

Whilst you can't push your staging date back to a later date you can bring your staging date forward and therefore start to comply with the regulation earlier than you need to.

Bringing your staging date forward might not be right for you, and if you're less than a year away from your staging date it might be worth spending the additional time planning to comply successfully once your staging date arrives.

However bringing your staging date forward and complying early can be useful for a number of reasons.

Firstly complying with auto enrolment regulation is a positive way to show your employees you're not only complying with the 'letter of the law' but willing to use these new obligations as an opportunity to make provisions sooner rather than later.

Secondly it's important to remember that you're not alone when it comes to the need to comply with auto enrolment rules.

Over the next couple of years there are hundreds of thousands of employers who also need to comply.

Whilst no one's entirely sure of the impact this is going to have on the market at this stage many people who have looked at the marketplace have fears that there is going to be a 'capacity crunch'.

For you as an employer this might mean that due to the demand for pensions, professional support to help you comply and the systems you might want to use to help you comply with auto enrolment will be far greater over the next couple of years.

Therefore staging early has another clear benefit.

If you decide to stage early, and before the period of time when hundreds of thousands of fellow businesses are trying to comply it's likely you'll have potentially a lot more choice.
A lot more choice when it comes to selecting the right pension for your employers.

A lot more choice when it comes to seeking and attaining professional advice.

A lot more choice when it comes to selecting the appropriate systems within your business to help you comply.

Now the reality is that 'capacity crunch' has seemed to be overcome by both the professional community, pensions provides and payroll professionals (and software firms) raising their game.

However we'll know more of whether capacity crunch is a real fiction or reality near the end of 2017.

Thirdly, staging early allows employers to get used to paying contributions at a lower rate.

Many employers over the next couple of years will stage on contribution levels higher than they are currently (more on the dates when this will increase later).

Staging early allows employers to start the auto enrolment process at lower levels and therefore allow employers to have a more gradual transition to the higher level of contributions.

Now if you do decide to stage early there's a few things worth bearing in mind…

When it comes to picking a date you can only select a date which is an existing staging date. This usually means it'll be the first of the month.

To ensure you've got enough time to comply successfully it's worth, even when you intend to bring your staging date forward, leaving yourself with enough time to fully meet your obligations.

Next, once you've decided that you want to stage early, you need to let the pensions regulator know of your intention to do so.

Bringing your staging date forward is a relatively easy process.

A quick Google search of "Bringing your staging date forward" should get you to the right page on the pension regulators website . Alternatively the link below will get you there[8].

From there complete the instructions to bring your staging date forward.

Points of contact / Assigning responsibility

The next important point for business owners and employers to consider is who's going to manage auto enrolment within their business.

Most businesses have someone who is a good project manager. Good at getting tasks done quickly and efficiently. Good at organising, collating and interpreting information.

---

[8] For more information on how to bring your staging date forward go to http://www.thepensionsregulator.gov.uk/employers/bringing-your-staging-date-forward.aspx)

For most businesses this person is the most appropriate person to manage your automatic enrolment project.

Whilst assigning someone internally to manage the auto enrolment project is important you also need to let the pensions regulator know who's going to be managing auto enrolment within your business.

This is so the regulator can send any of the required documentation through to the right person in your business.

The process of doing this is called 'nominating a contact' and the person within your business who is managing auto enrolment is called the 'primary contact'.

It's also worth letting the pensions regulator know whether you're working with a professional as you can also assign as a 'secondary contact' who will also receive a copy of the important documents relating to your business.

Again to find out how to do this you can either Google "Pensions regulator nominate a contact" or alternatively use the link at the bottom of this page[9].

Confirming who might need to be enroled

After you've worked out your staging date, decided whether to bring that staging date forward and then nominated a primary contract within your business (and a secondary professional contact as appropriate) the next step is to understand a little about how you're business is being specifically impacted.

---

[9] For more information on nominating a contact go to
https://automation.thepensionsregulator.gov.uk/Nomination

To do this you need to take a look at your workforce but before we start looking at spreadsheets containing information about your employees let me tell you a little bit about how different members of your team are impacted by auto enrolment in different ways.

Broadly speaking there are three categories of workers and how they are treated broadly depend on two things..

Firstly how old your workers are

and

Secondly how much they earn.

So, let's explore the different types of workers and how they're defined...

Eligible Jobholders (EJ)

They earn over the 'earnings trigger' (£10,000 in 2016/2017)

They are aged over 22 and have not yet reached the state pension age.

Non Eligible Jobholders (NEJ)

They earn more than the 'lower threshold' (£5824 in 2016/2017)

but

They don't fit into the "Eligible Jobholders" category (i.e. they are either younger than 22, over the state pension age or earn less than the earnings trigger - £10,000 in 2016/2017)

Entitled workers (EW)

They are workers who earn less than the 'lower threshold' (£5824 in 2016/2017)

Now different categories of workers are treated under the auto enrolment rules in different ways.

Eligible Jobholders need to be automatically enrolled into a scheme and are entitled to the employer contribution if they decide to continue to be part of the scheme (i.e. don't opt out)

Non Eligible Jobholders don't need to be automatically enrolled into a scheme. Although non eligible jobholders are not enroled, if they want to be part of the pension scheme they can choose to join and are entitled to an employer contribution.

Entitled workers don't need to be automatically enrolled into a scheme but need to be given access to a scheme if they choose to join one. However entitled workers aren't entitled to any employer contribution.

Once you know who within your business sits into what category this allows you to make a few calculations….

Understanding who within your business who might be eligible and non-eligible jobholders (and knowing that it's likely as an employer you'll be making contributions on their behalf for the lion's share of these people) allows you to calculate how much as an employer you'll have to contribute into your workforces pension scheme.

However it's important to be clear. Regardless of the number of eligible jobholders, non-eligible jobholders and entitled workers you've got within your business the obligations on you as an employer don't change. As long as you employer (with a few minor exemptions) you still need to comply.

As long as you employ (with a few minor exemptions) you still need to comply regardless of how many workers you have in each category.

Also, for most businesses, the number of different categories of workers will change over time.

The calculations on who fits into each category needs to happen during every payroll period (for example, if you pay your staff monthly these calculation needs to be completed on a monthly basis) however any decent payroll software package worth its salt can help you achieve this (more on software later).

However the idea of understanding the three different categories and how they are treated gives you a decent idea of what auto enrolment will cost you in pension contributions.

So, now you've got a decent idea of how much your pension contributions might be so you can plan for your business, and you've established that as part of your plan, let's move onto what you need to do to check whether your existing pension is 'fit for purpose' (if you've got one) or selecting a new scheme.

Also, for most businesses, the number of different categories of workers will change over time. The calculations on who fits into each category needs to happen at during every payroll period (for example, if you pay your staff monthly these calculation needs to be completed on a monthly basis) however any decent payroll software package worth its salt can help you achieve this (more on software later).

Employment contracts

One of the areas which are most ignored when it comes to auto enrolment compliance is when something stated in employment contracts conflict directly with the automatic enrolment legislation

You see, every employee within your business should have a contract of employment. This contract of employment may have conditions relating to pension entitlement.

In our experience many of the contracts we've reviewed on behalf of employers either have no mention of pensions, or alternatively have a specific pension clause which states a minimum period of employment before an individual is entitled to join the pension scheme.

Many of the minimum period of time (which is normally in line with their particular businesses probationary periods) is greater than 3 months.

However it's important to remember that when a new employee starts within your business you can only use postponement (we'll talk about this in more detail later) for a 3 month period.

As an example, let's say that ABC ltd had a clause contained within their employment contract which stated that their employees were entitled to access to a pension scheme after a 6 month probationary period.

However automatic enrolment legislation states that an employee can opt to join a pension scheme at any time (from their first day) and if they are an eligible worker (and therefore needs to be automatically enrolled) this can only be postponed for a maximum of 3 months.

Therefore ABC ltd have a problem. Their employment contracts say one thing and automatic enrolment legislation tells them to do something else. So what do they do?

The short answer is to change employment contacts in order to meet and comply with automatic enrolment legislation.

However there a number of things you need to consider.

Now I'm not an employment lawyer.

Therefore it made sense to ask Vandana Dass of Davenport Solicitors who are specialists in employment law to share both her knowledge and expertise on what to consider when reviewing your contracts.

You can find her explanation of what you need to consider and do in Appendix ii of this book.

Raising awareness of automatic enrolment

In our experience one of the best things you can do to ensure automatic enrolment is a success in your business is to keep your staff fully informed as early as possible when it comes to automatic enrolment.

This might raise a question in your mind…why does keeping your workforce fully informed of what you're doing become so powerful? There's actually a few reasons.

Firstly, and I'm conscious I'm probably not telling you something you don't already know, if you're working with a team of employees within your business you'll get the most out of them if they feel actively engaged in your business.

I'm lucky enough to work with a bunch of really successful businesses.

The businesses, large and small, who run most smoothly and successfully, have committed teams of people who feel engaged in the work they do, understand the vision for the organisation moving forward and where they are not only financially but also emotionally engaged in the success of your business.

Building this emotional engagement within your business can be done in a bunch of different ways and there's plenty of books which will help you build this culture within your business (my favourite is Drive by Daniel Pink, but there's plenty of others) however one of the most powerful ways in our experience is to ensure employers understand upcoming changes which will impact both your business and employees.

Automatic Enrolment is one of these changes.

Raising awareness of automatic enrolment as early as possible is therefore an important action to ensure that you can answer queries from your team with plenty of time to spare, engage your team in helping you make choices you need to make about the automatic enrolment process and allow your employees plenty of time to make decisions about their own personal retirement needs.

Now it's important to mention that whilst that I've included 'raising awareness' in the chapter on regulation and whilst it is an action designed to make your automatic enrolment process easier it isn't a requirement under the law governing automatic enrolment legislation.

However it is considered to be really good practice to let your team know about these changes as early as possible[10].

<u>Choosing the definition of pensionable salary</u>

Okay before you read this let me make a suggestion..

---

[10] For more information on raising awareness with staff please go to http://www.thepensionsregulator.gov.uk/employers/raising-awareness-about-automatic-enrolment.aspx

Before getting stuck into this section get yourself a nice cup of tea, glass of wine, large scotch, gin & tonic (my particular tipple of choice)!

Understanding this aspect of automatic enrolment and making a decision in this area, even for professionals who work in our sector, is in our experience one of the most challenging elements when navigating the automatic enrolment process.

Right, have you got your beverage of choice sitting next to you? Let's begin....

All employers, large or small, need to decide on what their level of contribution into the pension scheme is going to be and how that's going to be defined.

On the next couple of pages you'll find tables highlighting the choices employers have when picking contributions (along with the minimum contribution levels for both employers and employees required between now and when automatic enrolment is rolled out to all existing employers and some new ones in 2018)

However it's not as easy as selecting the lowest percentage levels and immediately getting the most cost effective option for your business.

To understand the options you've got when it comes to contribution levels please take a look at the tables and read the following few pages before making a choice.

Qualifying earnings

Date	Employer Minimum Contribution	Total Minimum Contribution
Until 5th April 2018	1%	2%
6th April 2018 – 5th April 2019	2%	5%
6th April 2019 onwards	3%	8%

Percentage of pensionable pay ('SET 1')

Date	Employer Minimum Contribution	Total Minimum Contribution
Until 5th April 2018	2%	3%
6th April 2018 – 5th April 2019	3%	6%
6th April 2019 onwards	4%	9%

Percentage of pensionable pay (if pensionable pay is at least 85% of total pay) ('SET 2')

Date	Employer Minimum Contribution	Total Minimum Contribution
Until 5th April 2018	1%	2%
6th April 2018 – 5th April 2019	2%	5%
6th April 2019 onwards	3%	8%

Percentage of Total pay ('SET 3')

Date	Employer Minimum Contribution	Total Minimum Contribution
Until 5th April 2018	1%	2%
6th April 2018 – 5th April 2019	2%	5%
6th April 2019 onwards	3%	7%

We'll talk about how you calculate total pay, pensionable pay and qualifying earnings in a minute however first let's explore what the two percentage rates mean.

First you've got 'employer minimum contribution'.

That's the percentage this particular employer pays into their employees' pension scheme.

Then you've got total minimum contribution.

This is the amount, as a minimum, which needs to go into the pension scheme as a total.

This includes both the employers contribution and the employees contribution.

So if a total minimum contribution is 2% and the employer's minimum is 1% then it makes sense that the extra 1% we need to get to the minimum comes from the employee.

As you can see from October 2018 onwards the contribution levels are between a 8% - 9% total minimum and a 3 – 4% minimum employer contribution.

Therefore it's important as a business to plan for this increase in contributions as well as communicating with your employees that there contributions will also increase over time to meet the statutory minimum levels.

How is pensionable pay, total pay and qualifying earnings calculated

Pensionable pay is calculated at the discretion of the business owner.

Usually pensionable pay usually includes just basic pay but not overtime or bonuses.

Total pay is all your staff's earnings including salary (or wages), commission, bonuses, overtime, statutory sick pay & statutory maternity pay.

Qualifying earnings (the basis on which most employers select) is worked out differently.

It's the earnings for all members of your team between £5824 and £42,835 (in the tax year 2015/2016)

If you use the qualifying earnings definition you need to include the following when calculating:-

Salary
Wages
Commission
Bonuses
Overtime
Statutory sick pay
Statutory maternity pay
Statutory paternity pay (ordinary or additional)
Statutory adoption pay

Now there might be elements of pay for your workforce which sit in a 'grey area'. An area where they are difficult to place in one of the categories above.

Typical examples of might be car or clothing allowance, travel allowance, regional weighting (extra pay for being based in a certain area) and/or allowance for food or phones although there might be others.

If an element of your employees pay include some of these 'grey area' payments you can decide not to include these parts of pay when you're working out pension payments however you need to include all of the elements of pay (salary, wages, commission....etc.) on the list above.

By now you've probably finished the first glass or cup of your beverage of choice.

However can I suggest you top up your glass as now you need to decide, having read about the different definitions, on how to work out the best definition for you.

For most employers it's most cost effective to opt to calculate their pension contributions using "qualifying earnings" when working out their pension contributions.

However on occasions (in particular when your business only pays Salary with no additional benefits or alternatively pays significant amount of bonuses, commission and overtime) that one of the other methods of working out how you're going to work out your pension contributions might be more appropriate.

To calculate the best option for you, and if you're quite handy with spreadsheet software, you can work out what the most cost effective option for you is going to be.

Alternatively, your payroll software might be able to calculate the best basis to calculate your contributions but not all payroll software providers do this.

Due to the fact that we understood the challenge of working this out, we have also built a contributions calculator on AE in a Box which helps employer users calculate the most appropriate selection for them.

This means that AE in a Box users have an easy way to calculate the most appropriate contribution level for their business.

What's next?

Once you've decided the way you're going to work out your pension contributions, you need to do a couple of things.

Firstly you need to put on file how you're going to work out pension contributions and secondly you need to confirm with your payroll software of choice (or middleware if you've decided to use it) the options you've selected so they can process the payments efficiently.

However before you pour your third drink (you might need it by now), there is something you should know which might make your life in this regard far easier…

The ways of working out contributions I've detailed above are the statutory minimums. Many employers we work with, instead of going through the complexity of calculating certification take a simpler more straightforward approach.

In our experience there are a decent number of employers who pay a percentage over and above the legal minimum on their employees.

For example, many employers who have decided to pick the "qualifying earnings" definition who instead of paying contributions between the two bands at the percentage rates detailed above go for a far simpler solution.

For example they may decide to pay 2% (or often 3 or 4%) employer contributions on all earnings and ask their employees to pay the same with an understanding that this will need to increase over time to meet the increasing minimums.

This amount currently exceeds the statutory minimum based on the "qualifying earnings" definition and therefore means that an employer is meeting their obligations under automatic enrolment, This is potentially easier for you and your employees to understand and simplifies how contributions are worked out.

Therefore that simple approach (a percentage of everything an employee earns), as long as the contribution levels always exceed the statutory minimum might be the most appropriate way forward for your business.

Postponement

As an employer, when it comes to automatically enrolling your employees into the scheme you've got a choice of when you automatically enrol them into your scheme, effectively delaying what employees you need to automatically enrol in by up to three months.

The option to be able to delay automatically enrolling individuals into your pension scheme is called postponement.

When it comes to postponement you'll need to decide whether to use this rule in two areas.

Firstly whether you postpone automatically enrolling existing employees when you reach your staging date and secondly whether you postpone automatically enrolling new employees when they join your business after your staging date.

Now, before we take a look at how postponement works in practice, I want to be clear about what postponement isn't.

Postponement isn't a way to defer your staging date.

If you decide to use postponement you're deciding to postpone when you automatically enrol employees into your scheme, not deferring your obligations under the law.

Therefore on most occasions you still need to have a pension scheme in place on your staging date,
You still need to let employees into a scheme and make contributions on their behalf on your staging date if they decide to opt into the scheme prior to postponement

Also you still need to communicate with your employees prior to your staging date as well as all of the other obligations you've got under the new law as well as letting your employees know that you intend to postpone automatically enrolling them.

Postponement doesn't allow you to defer your obligations by putting your staging date back for three months but simply provides an opportunity for not automatically enrolling employees immediately on staging date (or alternatively when they join your business).

So, let's look at a practical example….

Postponement – A practical example

TRF Design Ltd have 8 employees of whom all of them are entitled workers (and therefore need to be automatically enrolled in the pension scheme.

They have a staging date of the 1st August 2016. They understand that they need to have a pension scheme in place, communicate with their workers explaining the new rules and meet all of their additional obligations under the new rules.

However they have heard about postponement and wonder how it applies to them[11].

They decide that they want to postpone automatically enrolling their workers for 3 months.

They ensure they let their workers know by telling them they intend to postpone automatically enrolling them for 3 months and ensure that they let their payroll software know they intend to postpone.

They also set a pension up in plenty of time and meet all of their additional obligations which they must complete by their staging date regardless of using postponement or not.

When their staging date arrives, 2 of their employees decide they want to join the pension scheme immediately instead of waiting for the three month period.

THF Design, having understood that if any staff within their business they have the right to do this, put them in the pension scheme and start deducting employee contributions (as well as paying employer contributions on their behalf) from day one.

After three months the remaining employees are automatically enroled into the scheme.

---

[11] For more details on postponement go to
(http://www.thepensionsregulator.gov.uk/employers/postponement.aspx)

THF Design also decide that they for new employees joining the business after their staging date they will use postponement so that any new starters aren't automatically enroled in immediately.

In September 2016 they have a new starter, Jeff (who as an entitled worker needs to be automatically enroled)

Jeff is put on the payroll system and after 3 months is automatically enroled into the/ scheme.

Why you might decide to use postponement

There are a number of reasons why you might decide to use postponement within your business.

Firstly many businesses use it to try to reduce the upfront costs of the new regulation. If you're employees don't opt in early and instead wait three months before they decide to opt in you've saved yourself three months' worth of pension contributions.

For many businesses this amount might be relatively small. For some businesses this might be a decent chunk of cash However it's worth working out and seeing if the value of saving the pension contributions is enough of an incentive to postpone when you opt in employees.

Please bear in mind though that it's important to remind you that if employees want to go in prior to the 3 month postponement period you need to let them enter the scheme early and assist them to do this.

Secondly many employers use postponement, especially for their new employees to ensure that there is a delay between when new employees start and when they go into the pension scheme.

Before the new legislation many employers used to have a probationary period before they let new employees join their pension scheme.

Typically this used to range from 1 month to 6 months.

Whilst employers now can't defer pension contributions for 6 months (the maximum postponement under the new rules is 3 months) they can use postponement for their new employees so that they employees aren't placed into a scheme immediately but after the postponed period.

One important point here is when your business has an existing contract of employment which states a 6 month probation as standard with entry into the pension after this period of time.

Obviously this directly conflicts with the new automatic enrolment rules and therefore it's worth consulting with an employment lawyer to confirm what changes need to be made in this regard.

As mentioned already there's specific support on this particular subject written by Vandana Dass from Davenport solicitors in appendix ii of this book.

Thirdly, if you run a business with individuals who come and work for you for a short period of time (three months of less) you may not want to enrol these individuals immediately knowing that they intend to work on a short term project with you and then leave.

Therefore postponement means that you don't need to immediately put these individuals into a scheme, and if they leave prior to the 3 month period, at all.

However it's important to remember that if they continue being employer in your business you will need to automatically enrol them if they qualify.

What you need to do if you want to postpone

The process of postponement is relatively easy.

First you need to decide whether postponement is right for your business and then whether you're going to use postponement for existing employees when approaching your staging date, for new employees when starting employment after you staging date, or both existing and new employees.

Secondly you need to communicate with your staff about your decision to postpone. There are template communications to help you do this available on the pension regulators website.

Then you need to let the software you've decided to use (be it either independent 'middleware' or payroll software) to process your pension payments and calculate what needs to be paid when.

There's no need to notify the regulator at the date of postponement, although it's important to keep a record of when and why you've postponed[12].

Opting in

Anyone of your employees can opt in.

Eligible workers, if you've decided to use postponement, can decide to opt in prior to the postponement period ending.

Non eligible workers aren't automatically enroled into the scheme but can choose to opt in at any time.

---

[12]For more detailed information on postponement you can find the pension regulators guidance here
http://www.thepensionsregulator.gov.uk/employers/postponement.aspx

It's also important to remember that non eligible workers are also entitled to receive the minimum employer contribution from you but are obliged to contribute the minimum by law too.

Entitled workers are entitled to join the pension scheme and can contribute but aren't entitled to contributions from their employer.

(if you need a reminder who constitutes Eligible, Non Eligible and Entitled workers take a look at page 78)

As an employer if anyone from your workforce decides they want to opt in you need to help them do this.

Opting out

It's important to remember that any one of your employees, once they've been automatically enroled in can decide to opt out.

Therefore you need to, as part of your communication process let employees know they're entitled to opt out.

It's important to remember that employees who decide to opt out do need to be opted back in every three years.

Also, this three year anniversary isn't the anniversary of when the employee has decided to opted out but the three year anniversary of the staging date.

Practically it looks like this…

A short 'opting out' case study

Roy runs a business with 10 employees with a staging date of 1st April 2016.

Two of those employees opted out of the pension scheme, one in September 2016 and one in October 2016. On 1st April 2019 Roy will need to opt the two employees who have opted out back in together with anyone else who has opted out in the meantime.

How does opting out work practically?

For employees to opt out they need to complete a document which contains the following information:-

The name of the employer

The name of the employee

The employee's date of birth or national insurance number
The date the form was completed

It needs to be signed, or if held electronically, confirmation that the employee submitted the request.

It also needs to include the three following statements:-

"I wish to opt out of pension saving"

"I understand that if I opt out I will lose the right to pension contributions from my employer"

"I understand that if I opt out I may have a lower income when I retire"

Also, the opt out notice needs to contain a section (called 'what you need to know') which contains the following information:-

Your employer cannot ask you or force you to opt out

If you are asked or forced to opt out, you can tell the pensions regulator

If you change your mind, you may be able to opt back in

If you change your job your new employer will normally put you back into pension saving straight away.

If you have another job, your other employer might also put you into pension saving, now or in the future.

This notice only applies to the employment you have with the employer named on this notice. A separate notice must be filled out and given to any other employer you work for, if you wish to opt out of saving in that scheme as well.

Next, once the employee completed a document and hands it into you you'll need to notify both your payroll software together with your pension provider to confirm this opt out is registered and no additional contributions are to be taken.

If an employee decides to opt out after a month of being opted in all you'll need to do is stop future contributions (until they get auto enroled back in at the three year anniversary)

However if an employee decides to opt out within a month of being opted in you'll need to stop future contributions and arrange a refund of any contributions they've paid.

You should be able to do this with ease with the pension provider you've selected to administer your scheme.

However remember, and your payroll software should be able to help you with this, you need to re-enrol this individual every three years.

Inducements

If you're an employer there's one thing you should totally avoid when thinking about opt outs and that's getting involved with persuading employees to opt out.

Employers persuading employees to opt out, either by putting in place incentives (for example an increase in salary or other benefits) or verbally (i.e. "I tell you what mate, I'd opt out of that pension scheme if I were you") are opening themselves to a decent amount of liability.

If you're found to have induced your employees to opt out of the pension scheme you could be liable for a decent amount in fines as well as the potential risk of employee tribunals if one of your employees become disgruntled.

So, inducing your employees in any way shape or form is bad news and is to be avoided as an employer at all costs.

However this raises an issue.

If you've issued the statutory communications letting employees know that they're going to be automatically enroled into a pension scheme and they come to you for some guidance in what to do.

Namely, how can you deal with this without later being accused of inducing your employees to opt out.

Many employers decide to work with a professional who can come in and explain the options employees have however there are more cost effective ways to deliver impartial and independent communications to your workforce.

Some of the automatic enrolment support solutions provide help in a low cost effective way designed to help you communicate to your employees.

For example "AE in a Box" provides a whole range of videos designed to help your employees understand how automatic enrolment impacts them and is designed to empower employees to make their own choices independent of any employer influence.

Communicating with your workforce

As an employer you've got to let your workforce know how automatic enrolment applies to them and whether you've decided to use postponement, or not.

The minimum legal obligation is that you write to your staff within 6 weeks after your staging date to confirm your obligations and their options and you can use the template letters which will help you do this on the pension regulators website[13].

Although the minimum legal standard is to issue this communication at least 6 weeks after your staging date there is value in considering issuing these documents sooner rather than later.

In our experience, most employers we've worked with find it easier to communicate with their teams prior to their staging date as opposed to waiting after the staging date.

One is for employees who need to be automatically enroled and the other for employees who don't need to be enroled and once you know who in your business sits in each category you can issue the right document to individual members of your staff as appropriate.

Bear in mind that you may have staff which start the automatic enrolment process as an individual who doesn't need to enroled immediately but can change (due to an increase in pay or the fact that they reach an age when they need to be automatically enroled).

Therefore you need to check during each and every payroll period if this occurs.

---

[13] For more information on how to write to your staff go to (http://www.thepensionsregulator.gov.uk/employers/write-to-your-staff.aspx)

In reality your payroll software if it has full automatic enrolment functionality may manage the communications process as part of its service.

However it's important to check if your payroll software does the job when it comes to communications and keeps an eye out for changes in the workforce so that it can issue new communications.

Alternatively if your payroll software doesn't offer communications you'll need to complete this process manually both up front and then keep an eye on changes in your workforce when the following occurs:-

You have a new starter where you need to issue new communications
You have someone who reaches the age where they need to be automatically enroled

You have someone where in a particular payroll period they exceed the amount the need to earn (the automatically enrolment trigger) which means they need to be automatically enroled.

It's also important to bear in mind that your own personal trigger (which works out to £10,000 annually in 2015/16) depends on how often you pay your employees[14].

In practice this means that if you pay someone monthly, and they usually earn £700 per month but (usually due to overtime, a bonus, or commissions) they earn more than £833 (the earnings trigger if you pay your workforce monthly) then they need to be both communicated with and also automatically enroled.

---

[14] You can find out the particular triggers dependent on frequency of payment here http://www.thepensionsregulator.gov.uk/employers/automatic-enrolment-earnings-threshold.aspx

It's also important to keep records of how you've communicated to each employee so that if the regulator ever wants to check how you've communicated to your workforce you're able to provide a decent amount of evidence.

Registering with the regulator

After you've done everything you need to so that you've complied with automatic enrolment you need to let the pension regulator know that you've done this.

The pensions regulator calls this registration the 'declaration of compliance' which effectively lets the regulator know that you've complied.

However before you complete your declaration of compliance you'll need to ensure you've signed up for a government gateway ID

The 'government gateway ID' allows you to sign up to register for a wide range of electronic services provided by the government including having access to a bunch of HMRC services, applying for driving licenses online as well as a wide range of other services which are used in areas as diverse as cattle movement reporting (nope, me neither!), state pension forecasts and parents who manage their child maintenance payments online.

It's likely that you've already got a government gateway ID, either managed by you or via your accountant as many of the HMRC online submissions are already completed via the government gateway.

So the first port of call, if the government gateway ID doesn't ring a bell, is to check with your accountant to confirm if you've already got a login.

Also if you've only got an individual government gateway you'll need to apply for a new one for your organisation as you need to register your business with the regulator (as opposed to you as an individual)

If you haven't got a login to this system, it's relatively easy to apply[15]:

However, let me provide you with a word of warning….

There are a few employers who have failed to comply (and therefore have been fined) as they assumed they had registered with the regulator but had only completed the government gateway application.

Applying for the government gateway is only the first stage of the process and you still need to complete your registration with the regulator after registering on the government gateway.

Registering for the government gateway is just that, a registration for a login. It doesn't mean that you've completed registering with the regulator (which is our next step).

Once you've got your government gateway you need to register with the regulator[16]:

However before you start to do this you'll need to know what information you need to comply successfully.

Luckily there's a checklist you can find on the pension regulators website which details what you need to comply[17].

---

[15] To apply for a login to the government gateway go to http://www.gateway.gov.uk/
[16] To register with the regulator please go to https://www.autoenrol.tpr.gov.uk/
[17] For more information on the checklist you can find on the pension regulators website which details what you need to comply please go to

Increasing contributions when the time is right

As I mentioned earlier in this book your contributions need to increase over time.

You can find out about when and by how much you need to increase contributions (and how you select the right contribution levels for your business) by reading about certification and contribution levels earlier in this chapter.

It's important you keep track of when you've got to increase your contribution levels to the new statutory minimum at the right times and keeping track of the appropriate dates.

As I write this the increase in contribution levels have been established up to October 2018 however one of the things which isn't clear at this stage is how contributions will increase after this.

It's therefore important to keep track of how and when contribution levels will change after that. You can either keep track of required changes in contribution levels after this stage by keeping on top of communications from the regulator or using an automatic enrolment support service to keep you informed of any future changes.

However to ensure you continue to remain compliant you need to make sure that the pension contributions increase over time as stipulated by law.

Keeping records

---

http://www.thepensionsregulator.gov.uk/employers/automatic-enrolment-registration.aspx

One of the important elements of ensuring you comply with the new legislation is ensuring you keep records.

There are a number of important pieces of information you need to keep on file as the regulator reserves the right to check your records at any time.

It's best practice to retain your records for automatic enrolment for as long as possible to provide a decent audit trail however you need to ensure you retain records for at least 6 years to comply with the new regulation (however if any of your staff opt out you only need to keep their opt out notices for 4 years as a minimum).

The information you should keep records on are:-

The names and addresses of everyone you've enrolled - you should have these records both on your payroll software and on the data you (or your payroll software) send to your pension provider. However it's worth keeping a backup on file of your own as a backup.

Records of contributions made and then they were paid - Again this information should be stored as part of your payroll software and the information you send to your pension provider.

However I'd also suggest that you keep your own backup as an additional way of keeping the data in case you decide to change either your pension or payroll software providers in the future.

Any opt-in and opt-out requests - These documents won't usually be uploaded onto your payroll software or part of your pension as they're likely to be handed to you directly.
Therefore it's important you need to have an independent way to store these requests safely and securely on your own systems.

Your pension scheme reference - This is an easy one. Your pension scheme reference number can be accessed via your pension provider, should be held on your payroll software.

Any information and data you send to your pension provider – Although your pension provider should be able to recall any information you send to them I'd also suggest that you keep a backup copy to ensure you're always in a position where you've got the information to hand if the pension regulator ever comes calling.

It's important to keep these records for your business. Not being able to supply these records when appropriate could result in fines.

Effectively keeping records under the automatic enrolment rules proves you're complying if the pension regulator ever decides to pay you a visit. Therefore it's fundamental that you keep decent records in all the areas we've mentioned above.

Ensuring you continue to comply with your automatic enrolment duties

As an employer there's a number of duties you need to comply with on an ongoing basis.

Firstly we've got the obligations I've talked about earlier in this book.

You need to re-enrol employees who have opted out every three years, increase contribution levels at the times the legislation dictates and in addition to this you have the option if appropriate to change the way you calculate contributions within your scheme.

You also, as we discussed already, need to process your payroll monthly and keep an eye of any of your employees who whilst not automatically enroled initially may need to be automatically enroled if their income increases above the minimum threshold or reaches the age of 22.

However the reality is that as I write this nobody knows the scope and scale of the tasks you'll need to complete as a business owner in the future.

The law that governs automatic enrolment, whilst being in the planning stages for a number of years and working in practice since 2012, is still in its relative infancy.

This means as this law continues to be implemented, and especially as it's implemented across the huge amount of SME employers over the next few years, there's a distinct possibility that the rules governing automatic enrolment might change to either clarify the rules, make it easier for employers to comply or react for feedback from a range of sources.

Also, when automatic enrolment is fully rolled out across the country and is impacting every existing and most new employers in the land (which is scheduled to happen in 2018) there's currently no guessing what the next changes to the law will be.

Perhaps the government will slowly increase contributions. Perhaps the pensions regulator will change some of the rules.

Perhaps the information you need to report to the regulator and the way you report this information will change. Perhaps the way you communicate to your employees will be amended.

The reality is at this stage currently we have no way of knowing what these changes are going to be. Also it's important to remember that complying with this legislation is for life, not just up to your staging date!

However this raises a question…

How do employers keep up to date with changes in regulation?

There's a few ways for employers to keep up to date with any changes in the rules governing automatic enrolment.

Firstly employers can sign up for the regulators email newsletter. This means that you'll get constant and regular updates from the regulator about a range of different topics relating to automatic enrolment.

Secondly, if you're working with your accountant, payroll bureau or financial planner on an ongoing basis you need to check that part of the service they're providing is to keep you fully informed and updated as and when changes occur.

This is important to check as some of the services provided by professionals are designed to ensure you comply just up to your staging date (instead of on an ongoing basis).

Thirdly you can use a commercial support service which is designed to provide constant and regular updates, together with the tasks you need as well as a wide range of other support services, to keep you fully informed and updated at every step of the way and ensuring you're fully informed of the actions you need to take. AE in a Box is one of the support services you can use to help you do this.

So, we've covered the most pertinent regulatory obligations you have under the automatic enrolment rules. Let's now explore the practical action you need to take in our 2nd circle – pensions.

Chapter 5

Pensions

The Second circle of Automatic Enrolment

As you'd probably expect from a set of rules designed to 'nudge' people into saving for their financial futures there needs to be, as part of the regulation, a place to put all of your employees money into.

Therefore, and again as you'd expect, having a suitable pension scheme is a fundamental part of the new regulation.

There is a number of factors to consider when it comes to selecting a suitable pension scheme for your employees.

However, let's start our journey through pension selection by considering an important factor...

Using an existing pension

Whilst there are a decent number of employers who haven't got a pension scheme which they might be able to use for automatic enrolment, there are a fair few businesses which already have a pension scheme of some description in place designed to encourage workplace savings.

This may be because they already contribute into a pension scheme for their employees or it might be that there is an old scheme which has never been used but has been set up.

It makes sense to think about whether, if you've got an existing scheme in place to use this as opposed to applying for a brand new scheme.

However first you need to check with the pension provider whether this scheme can be used to comply with automatic enrolment regulation.

So, If you've got an existing scheme you'll need to make a call to check whether your existing scheme is a qualifying scheme (i.e. can be used to comply with the automatic enrolment regulation) and armed with the questions below you'll be able to find out exactly whether you can use your old scheme or not.

Does your existing pension scheme allow new members and is it open to all?

The Auto Enrolment rules are designed to provide a way for everyone to save for their financial future. Therefore one of the core tenets of a qualifying auto enrolment scheme is that a qualifying workplace pension will allow new members and it's open to all.

Some pension providers are happy with opening up existing schemes to all of their members. Other pension providers have restrictions, normally in relation to minimum contribution levels, which mean that your particular scheme can't be open to all of your workforce.

Therefore this first thing you need to check and confirm with your pension provider is whether your existing scheme firstly allows new members and also whether the scheme is open to all.

If your existing scheme doesn't allow new members and isn't open to all it's likely the scheme isn't a qualifying scheme and therefore you'll need a new scheme to ensure you meet your auto enrolment obligations as an employer.

What's the annual management charge on your current scheme?

One of the important additional provisions of a 'qualifying scheme' under auto enrolment rules is that the annual management charge (the charge a pension scheme charges for administration and management) is below a certain limit.

Since April 2015, the maximum annual management charge is 0.75% however it's worth checking whether it's still at this level with the pensions regulator or a support service like AE in a Box if you're using one as this might have changed.

Therefore one of the important checks you need to make when it comes to seeing if your existing scheme charges less than this cap.

If it charges less than the cap....great!

If not you won't be able to use your existing scheme to comply with the auto enrolment regulation.

Does your existing scheme has a 'default' fund?

One of the key principals of the auto enrolment rules is that for employees to be auto enroled into a scheme they haven't got to make an immediate choice about where the money which is being saved is invested.

Therefore a qualifying pension scheme needs to have a fund to invest in which is a 'default'…..a fund which your employees money goes into if your employees don't make a choice.

Now many older pensions need individuals of the member scheme to make a choice and therefore can't be used under the automatic enrolment rules.

These schemes who need one of your employees to select a fund before going into the scheme won't be able to be used as an auto enrolment scheme.

Therefore you'll need to check with your existing pension provider, if you've got one, that there is a default fund for employees to enter in order for this particular scheme to comply with auto enrolment regulation. If not you won't be able to use this scheme to comply with auto enrolment regulation.

Does your existing scheme communicate to employees effectively?

There are an number of things an existing pension scheme must do in relation to communication to ensure it complies with auto enrolment regulation.

However before we talk about what your pension provider should do let's talk about communications in a little more depth.

Employers under the auto enrolment obligations have a duty to communicate these changes to their workforce, as well as communicate when that particular workers status changes.

Whilst your pension provider will communicate to your employees it's highly unlikely that it will do enough to meet your minimum obligations as an employer.

You see pension schemes need to send out new joiner packs, and annual statements which contain valuations, how the money is being invested and projections of a members pot.

We'll talk about the additional communication obligations you've got as an employer later in this book but for now just be clear that the pension provider has minimum obligations (shown above) but this doesn't fully meet all your compliance obligations and therefore shouldn't be used as your 'qualifying scheme'

The Final Check

If you've got this far and your existing scheme has confirmed they meet all the criteria above it's likely that you've got a scheme which you can use to comply with the auto enrolment scheme (bearing in mind that if your scheme can't complete even one of the above it shouldn't be used as a qualifying auto enrolment scheme).

However it's worth making a final check. Whilst you're on the phone to your pension provider and asking the questions, and assuming all the answers are yes, it's worth asking the 'final check' question from your pension provider....

"Can you confirm that our current scheme is a qualifying work place pension scheme and therefore can be used to meet my auto enrolment regulations?"

At this stage you'll know whether you can use your existing scheme or not....

However what happens if either you haven't got a scheme or you've worked out that your existing scheme isn't fit for purpose is you've got to pick a new qualifying workplace pension scheme...

Picking an auto enrolment pension scheme for your business

If you haven't got an existing scheme, or you've made the required checks and the existing scheme doesn't comply with auto enrolment regulation you've now got an additional task to complete....

You need to select an auto enrolment pension scheme for your business.

Selecting a pension scheme, if you haven't got an existing one which is compliant for your business, is an important part of the auto enrolment compliance process and you'll need to take care to ensure you select a pension which works for both your business and your employees.

Before we look at some of the factors you should consider, let's explore the three main methods you can use to select the most appropriate pension provider for your business.

1) Get Professional Advice

The traditional method of selecting a workplace pension provider is to seek advice from a professional who can conduct market research on your behalf and help you through the selection process.

Typically this professional is a fully qualified financial planner or adviser and they will usually assist you by understanding your needs as a business, conducting research in the marketplace and then coming back to you with the best fit for your business.

Whilst this is likely to be the most expensive option (compared to using a technology based support solution or making the decision yourself) many employers feel that consulting with a professional and having access to their experience and expertise in the market means that the choice they make is appropriate.

The choice to use a professional, instead of taking one of the alternative routes, to help you select an auto enrolment compliant pension is fundamentally up to you.

However it's important you conduct a degree of due diligence around the professional you choose to work with. With this in mind it's important to shop around and find out a little about the professional you intend to work with in these areas….

Qualifications

One of the first things to check when choosing the right professional to work with is to understand the particular professionals level of qualification.

If the professional you choose to work with is a financial adviser or planner they'll have minimum qualification standards they need to reach[18].

However it may be the case, as is becoming more common, that the professional who is recommending a pension may be your accountant, someone from your payroll bureau or an auto enrolment adviser who isn't affiliated to a particular professional body which demands minimum qualification standards..

In that case there's some value in asking some more questions of the professional about the qualifications which they feel make them capable of conducting robust and independent pensions research.

It's also worth checking, and especially if the professional you chose to work with is helping you with your additional auto enrolment duties, whether they have passed the Pensions Management Institute's certificate in auto enrolment.

---

[18] You can find out more about the different qualification standards for professionals here - https://www.unbiased.co.uk/ifa-qualifications

Experience

It's worth checking with your particular professional you intend to work with what experience they've had in the marketplace.

For example questions you might want to ask are

How many employers have they helped select pensions?

What challenges have they faced when helping employers selecting pensions?
How have they found the application process with different providers?

How have they helped employers like you?

Asking these questions will help you understand that the professional you are considering understands your needs and have helped employers like you in the past which will enable you to have far more confidence that the professional is making a choice which meets your needs.

Testimonials

Once you've got an indication of the experience of the professional you are considering to work with the next step is to ask about previous clients. A couple of questions you might want to consider are:-

Can you share some of your previous client testimonials?

Can I speak to some of your previous clients about their experience?

Research process

If you're paying a professional it's important to understand that they have a robust process in place in order to select the most appropriate auto enrolment pension scheme for you.

Some of the questions you might want to ask are:-

How will you find the right pension scheme for me?

What's your research process?

What tools do you use to help you with research and make your selection?

What validation will you give me to illustrate the process you've followed?

Fees (and Transparency)

Before you engage with any professional it's important to understand what and how you'll be paying for the service they provide.

Typically if a professional is only helping you with auto enrolment pension selection the odds are the service will be provided for a fixed fee.

It might be the case that the professional in question is providing additional services to you and your business where a retainer arrangement might be more appropriate.

However regardless of the charging structure of the particular professional you choose it's important that you're clear on what they charge and you consider it fair for both sides as well as understanding what the fee covers (for example does it cover the research process only or does it include research and application of the pension scheme)

We have seen examples of certain professionals deciding to partner up with one automatic enrolment pension scheme.

Whilst this approach might be suitable for some employers it's worth considering whether working with a professional who only recommends one pension solution instead of conducting a decent amount of research and selecting the most appropriate pension provider.

2) Use a 'support' service which helps guide you towards the most appropriate pension selection

Using a professional isn't the only way to select a qualifying workplace pension and we've seen a number of new style solutions for selecting a pension scheme pop up over the past year or so as more employers need to comply with auto enrolment legislation.

These solutions allow self-selection of a pension scheme but with support from a system which guides you through a process which makes pension selection easier.

Some of these systems are standalone where the sole purpose (for example the 'Pensions Playpen') however some have pension selection tools as part of a wider suite of auto enrolment support tools (like AE in a Box)
These solutions tend to be technologically based, lower cost than face to face advice but without the bespoke support which can be provided by having personal contact with a professional.

These sort of solutions are as I write this massively growing in popularity, particularly due to the fact that most smaller employers may not have the budget or inclination to pay a professional but feel they need additional help when selecting a pension. Therefore these solutions might be a feasible route to help you select a pension for your business.

3) Make the selection yourself by conducting your own research

If you decide that instead of working with a professional or using one of the available tools on the marketplace you want to conduct your own research and select a pension independently you can absolutely take this approach...

There are a number of factors worth considering when selecting a fully compliant pension scheme for your business. I've detailed below some of the most important factors you should consider when selecting a pension scheme but this list is by no means definitive.

I'm conscious that there may be other factors which are important to you and your business which you might want to check. Therefore it's worth using the factors below as a checklist to confirm you've thought about these factors when making your pension selection…

Does the pension provider provide a compliant auto enrolment scheme?

The tests which apply to existing pension providers in checking whether their scheme is compliant also apply to selecting a new pension provider.

After all, you don't want to select a new pension provider without first checking it meets the minimum requirements of an auto enrolment pension scheme.

These minimum requirements are the same for new schemes as they are for existing schemes and are detailed on page 109.

So, when selecting a new pension provider it's important to initially check that their particular schemes meet the minimum levels of compliance before looking at other factors….

How financially strong is the pension provider?

It's important you select a scheme you're confident is financially strong and therefore sustainable enough to provide a long term pension solution for both you and your employees.

Therefore one of the most important factors in selecting a pension provider is to find one which is financially strong (and therefore stable enough) to be the right home for your employees longer term savings.

For more traditional pension providers there are independent ratings on the financial strength of different pension provider. The easiest way of doing this is to google - "Pension Provider Financial Strength"

However many of the newer master trust pension arrangements (for example, NEST and The Peoples Pension) are not given financial strength ratings given out by the traditional rating companies like Standard & Poor and Moody's.

This doesn't necessarily mean they aren't financially strong it's just that they aren't analysed by these more traditional rating firms.

However it's relatively easy to get the information you need in order to understand how financially strong a particular master trust is.

Many master trust pension providers publish their accounts public and openly and usually you can find this on their website and there is currently more research being applied to these particular schemes which will eventually mean easier ways to judge their financial strength.

What are the costs of the pension provider for the employee?

One of the key factors in ensuring you select a good auto enrolment scheme is selecting one which doesn't charge the earth.

Ensuring your employees have confidence that you've selected a good scheme is tough to do and one of the easiest ways to erode this trust is to pick a scheme which charges too much.

Luckily (and as I've already mentioned) as of April 2015 there is a cap on what pension providers can charge annually. However there is still a decent amount of variation in the market on what pension providers charge.

Therefore it's important to understand how much the particular pension provider charges. For most pension providers they show this as an annual percentage charge (this is usually called the annual management charge).

However one note of caution. Whilst most pension providers just have an annual management charge there are providers which have charges on contributions as well as alternative ways of charging.

When deciding on the most appropriate scheme for your employees it's important to have a focus on the costs of any particular pension scheme.

Doing this, and especially if you communicate you've done this to your workforce, will ensure that your workforce can have confidence in the selection you've made.

Does the pension charge the employer?

Some schemes also charge the employer but provide additional services for this particular charge.

Employer charges are normally paid directly from the employer to the pension provider and usually the employer receives additional software, extra support or more choice to validate paying the additional amount.

In the first edition of this book I made the point that most pension providers don't charge the employer for pension set up. However the market has changed to the point where the majority of pension providers now charge you to set up your pension (with a couple of notable exceptions)

Whether they will charge depends on a number of factors however it's always worth checking before selecting a pension scheme whether that particular scheme will charge you if you're an employer.

How much fund choice does the particular pension provide?

As we've already mentioned, every auto enrolment pension scheme has to provide a 'default fund'. This default fund allows your employees to be put into the pension without making a specific choice.

However in our experience a fair few employees want to make an alternative choice and need access to a range of funds within the pension they can invest in.

Therefore before you select your auto enrolment pension fund it's worth considering how many alternative funds they offer and whether this choice of funds will be broad enough to provide a decent choice to the staff within your business.

Has the pension provider got a reputation for delivering good service?

The last thing you want when selecting a new pension scheme is to select that particular provider and find that they have shoddy service.

Auto Enrolment should be made as straightforward as it can be where possible and having a pension provider who provides a decent service is a key component to making the process easy.

Defaqto provide decent amounts of research into the service standards of different pension providers[19] but similarly to the

---

[19] For Defaqto service ratings go to

financial strength indicators don't always include the master trust pension arrangements (including NEST or the Peoples Pension).

However if you're considering a master trust arrangement help is at hand from the Pensions Quality Mark[20]

Also, and especially as we're approaching the market where hundreds of thousands of employers need to comply, it's worth when making your selection to keep an eye out in both the financial and mainstream press to see whether there are any stories of pension providers either doing a positive (or alternatively if you're looking for which pension providers to potentially avoid - negative) job for their customers as this might help you make your pension choice.

Is your payroll compatible with this particular pension provider?

One of the other factors to consider, especially when it comes to ensuring auto enrolment runs smoothly within your business is to ensure that you're payroll software (if you use one) is compatible with your pension provider.

We'll talk about this in a lot more depth later in this book. However suffice to say at this stage that it's worth checking with both your pension and payroll provider whether the data they both use are compatible with each other.

Does your pension provider allow transfers in and out?

---

https://www.defaqto.com/siteassets/financial-advisers/ratings/service-ratings/2015-pension-service-ratings-ch.pdf

[20] You can find more about a master trust arrangement here
http://www.pensionqualitymark.org.uk/pqmreadyschemes.php

One of the questions we often get asked, especially from employees who have been building pension pots independently of their employer or have built up pension pots historically with previous providers, is…

Can employees transfer their old pension pots into the new scheme you set up?

and

Can employees transfer the money they build up in their pension pots out to a different provider?

The answer is it depends on the particular pension provider. Most providers allow transfers in and out of their pension schemes however it's worth checking first with your employees whether they feel this is appropriate and then checking with the pension schemes you're considering whether transferring pension funds in and out to other pension providers is possible.

As you can see there are many factors to consider when selecting an appropriate pension for your workforce.

It's also a decision which is worth providing some thought to and ensuring that you're making the right selection for both you and your employees.

However by asking the questions above and making a decision on the information you'll receive you're more likely to select a scheme which is the right choice longer term for both you, your business and you're employees.

<u>Select and apply</u>

Once you've made your decision on who to use for your pension scheme the next step is to select and apply for the particular scheme.

Most automatic enrolment pension providers have online portals backed up by telephone support which allow you to apply pretty easily so the application process should be pretty straightforward.

Once the pension provider has confirmed that you've got a scheme in place ready for automatic enrolment you can then focus on ensuring your payroll software is fit for purpose.

Strangely enough, that's what we'll cover off in our next chapter....

Chapter 6

Payroll

The third circle of Automatic Enrolment

After selecting the most appropriate pension scheme the next step is to review how you manage payroll…

There are a number of factors to consider when considering how you manage payroll within your business and how to tailor payroll to ensure that the entire automatic enrolment process is as smooth as possible.

Also reviewing what your payroll software does and doesn't do is an important part of ensuring you can comply with auto enrolment successfully.

The reason for this is that if you're using the right software it can manage a lot of the regular tasks you need to conduct to ensure you comply with auto enrolment successfully and can help you automate many of the processes within your business.

If you or your payroll bureau doesn't use payroll software it's important to find out as early as possible prior to your staging date as you may decide to change your payroll software (or the bureau you use) to one which can help you save time and be more efficient.

Ideally you want a piece of payroll software which manages the ongoing automatic enrolment process. Alternatively you may decide to manually complete many of the automated tasks usually managed through payroll software.

Increasingly business owners and the professionals who work with them realise that trying to comply manually with automatic enrolment is a thankless task.

Whilst there is a cost to decent payroll software which automates much of the process it is minimal compared to the time spent trying to comply with automatic enrolment manually in businesses across the country.

When I wrote the first edition of this book (which was released in November 2015) I mentioned that the payroll software and bureau market was in a state of flux.

As I write this (in December 2016) the payroll software and bureau market have risen to the automatic enrolment set.

Whilst there are many exceptions (and it's important to bear in mind that there are hundreds of different types of payroll software) the majority of the large and now medium sized payroll software providers can support automatic enrolment relatively easily.

When it comes to payroll bureaus most of these businesses are also positioned to support employers, although it's important when deciding who to use to run your payroll that you understand their experience helping employers with automatic enrolment.

Although the market has moved on it's important not to assume that every single piece of payroll software or software bureau supports you with the tasks you need to complete...

It's therefore important to understand what your payroll software / bureau will do (and won't do) to help you comply with auto enrolment.

Therefore let's talk about some of the tasks some of the more comprehensive payroll software does to support you to comply with automatic enrolment on a regular basis and what you can do if it doesn't:-

Calculate during each payroll process who should be enrolled

Most payroll software geared to comply with auto enrolment should be able to take your payroll data and confirm every time you pay your workforce whether you have any new employees who should be enroled.

This process needs to be completed each and every time you pay your workforce due to the fact that employees who were previously non eligible or 'entitled' workers (i.e. not automatically enrolled) can turn into eligible workers (who need to be automatically enrolled).

This can happen for a couple of reasons, however one typical example is when an employee gets paid a bonus or has some overtime. Let me explain….

If one of your part time employees earns £700 per month (£8400 per annum) but one month earns £900 per month (£10,800 per annum and therefore over the 2015 threshold of £10,000 - see page 78) that particular individual then needs to be automatically enrolled in your pension scheme.

Therefore for many businesses both large and small, having your payroll do the calculations to see if any individuals have exceeded the threshold during every payroll period makes sense.

There are businesses with low staff turnover and stable salaries where this will be less of an issue however even within those companies new starters will need to be assessed when they come on board.

In our experience most payroll software with even a small degree of auto enrolment functionality will do this however please check with your payroll provider to see if this functionality is included.

If you're payroll doesn't do this you'll need to manage this process manually. This means that every time you pay your staff you'll need to 'assess' to see if there were any changes which mean some of your workforce need to be enrolled in.

However depending on the size and complexity within your business this could be quite an onerous task and therefore it's worth initially checking whether payroll can support you to do this[21]...

Calculate pension contributions during every payroll period

Once your payroll software has calculated who needs to be automatically enrolled the next step is for your payroll to calculate what the pension contributions will be.

Any decent payroll software will have the ability to calculate pension contributions depending on what percentages are selected however we're finding that on the odd occasion there are some pieces of payroll software which can't accommodate calculating pension contributions.

If I'm being perfectly Frank (although as a reminder - my name is still Chris!) if you're using a payroll provider without the ability to, as a minimum, calculate pension contributions complying with auto enrolment is going to be made far more complicated than it needs to be.

---

[21] For more information on the checks you need to make every time you pay your workforce you can take a look here http://www.thepensionsregulator.gov.uk/employers/check-who-you-need-to-enrol.aspx

Therefore it's worth checking and confirming that your payroll software can calculate pension contributions however as I've mentioned I'd be pretty surprised if it doesn't!

If you're existing payroll software doesn't do the job in this regard I'd humbly suggest that now would be an appropriate time to review your existing software and do a bit of research in the market to find a more appropriate payroll solution which performs this core task.

Whilst theoretically the process of calculating pension contributions manually can be done it complicates the process of compliance massively and therefore I'd suggest should be avoided in all costs.

In addition to the ability to calculate pension contributions the other thing you will want to check with your payroll provider is whether it updates the contribution percentages automatically when the legal minimum contributions levels increase (see page 84).

If your payroll software reminds you when contributions increase….great!

If not you can use a system like AE in a Box to remind you when you need to increase your contribution levels or alternatively build your own manual process to remind you of the changes in contribution levels.

Retain records for the pension regulator

One of the important things all employers need to do is to keep records of auto enrolment compliance if the pensions regulator ever needs to confirm and check whether you've complied.

Whilst all employers should be keeping independent records of what they've done in order to comply with auto enrolment there are a few payroll software tools which help you to do this.

We've covered off what information you need to retain for the pensions regulator in an earlier chapter[22]:

Much of the information employers need to retain they can do manually.

However especially if your payroll software deals with your communication process your payroll software would retain some of the records you need to keep to prove you've met your duties.

When it comes to retaining records for the pension regulator the reality is that employers will need to retain records in addition to the information your payroll software retains.

Therefore the key here is finding out how much information your payroll software retains on their systems, confirming what as an employer the records you need to retain and putting in place a manual solution to 'fill the gaps'.

Has the ability to 'talk to' your pension provider

Auto Enrolment is made easier by ensuring the processes you follow are as streamlined as much as possible.

In our experience where many employers find pain in the auto enrolment process is how payroll software produces information to send to the pension provider.

---

[22] For more details on records keeping go to
http://www.thepensionsregulator.gov.uk/employers/record-keeping.aspx

Let me explain how this works....

Let's say the information your payroll provider produces is in French. However your pension provider can only understand information which is in, erm I don't know, Japanese.

If this was the case what you might need is a way to translate French to Japanese otherwise the information sent from your payroll software to your pension will be lost in translation!

However if your payroll provider produces information in French but had the ability to translate it into Japanese before it was sent to the pension provider that would make your life a lot easier as you wouldn't have to worry about translation in the middle!

Practically this means that the formats of the information sent from the payroll software to the pension provider is in a format the pension provider can understand.

This means not *literally* translating from French to Japanese but matching the data if it doesn't match isn't far off!

Therefore it's important to ask your payroll software, having selected which pension you've opted to go for the following...

"Do you create and send a data file to (your pension provider) in a format they can understand?"

If your payroll software can do this job....great!

However if they can't there are two options in relation to this. Middleware software (more on this later) might be worth considering.

Alternatively you can translate the data manually from the language of the payroll software to the language of the pension provider although it's worth considering this might be a relatively time consuming and onerous task to complete.

Has the ability to re-enrol employees every three years

Most of the employees who decide to opt out of the auto enrolment pension scheme need to be 'nudged' back into the scheme every three years by law.

Many of the more sophisticated payroll software with auto enrolment functionality does this automatically although in our experience many of the payroll packages haven't included this as part of their functionality.
Therefore it's worth double checking whether your payroll software has this functionality.

If not you can use a compliance reminder service or put in place a manual process to remind you this needs to be done on a regular basis.

Issue the mandatory communications required under the auto enrolment rules

Under the auto enrolment regulation you need to issue certain mandatory communications to your workforce. For some of the larger payroll software providers they provide the functionality to produce and provide these documents through their platform.

Therefore it's worth checking with your payroll software provider whether it will issue the regulatory communications all employers have to issue.

If you're payroll software doesn't issue these communications you can meet your obligations to communicate with your employees manually[23]:-

The HMRC free payroll service

The reality is that whilst many SME businesses use commercial payroll software which will have decent levels of auto enrolment functionality (or alternatively work in partnership with a payroll bureau who uses decent payroll software) there are hundreds of thousands of businesses who continue to use the free PAYE service to manage their payroll.

The free tool available from the HMRC does a decent job in managing payroll however as I write this it has no auto enrolment functionality.

Now as I write this the pension regulator has announced they're developing some tools for users of the HMRC's free payroll service but it hasn't been confirmed what they'll do specifically or when they'll be launched.

If you've got a bit of time until your staging date you might be able to wait to see if the tools released by the pensions regulator can help you however for the purposes of this book I've had to assume, due to the fact we don't know when the pensions regulator will issue these support services, that you won't be using them.

So if you're using the HMRC payroll tool and intend to continue to use the HMRC payroll tool post your staging date you'll need to put manual processes (or use 'middleware' - more on this later) for

---

[23] For more information on what you need to do you can find details of your obligations here http://www.thepensionsregulator.gov.uk/employers/write-to-your-staff.aspx

all of the tasks the more sophisticated payroll software tools will complete on your behalf.

The decision to continue to use the free HMRC payroll service or not will depend on your business. However many SME employers are deciding that paid payroll software (or a payroll bureau) which manages many of the payroll elements of auto enrolment is a more appropriate way to go.

The reason? Whilst the more functional payroll software (or using a bureau) is obviously a more expensive route in cash terms, it could be a better route due to the time it'll save within your businesses due to the fact that many of the obligations are automated.

So if you're using the free HMRC tools you can continue to do this and meet your other obligations under auto enrolment manually or alternatively spend a few quid a month buying software which automates many of the processes.

The choice is yours.

Middleware

In the early days of auto enrolment (back in 2012) there were plenty of larger employers who needed additional software over and above their payroll software to help them comply with auto enrolment.

There were a couple of reasons for the need of additional software…

Firstly many of the payroll systems, which have since done massive amounts of work to build auto enrolment functionality, didn't help these larger businesses comply with auto enrolment and therefore needed help from this additional software.

Secondly the complexity of many of the larger businesses, who often had multiple pensions and payroll providers, meant that having an external piece of software designed to make these larger employers lives easier made sense.

The software which met these needs was called 'Middleware' and is still available in the marketplace to perform the same tasks (i.e. using technology fulfilling some of your duties if you're payroll software can't and having an external hub to manage complex arrangements)

We've seen a massive decrease of "middleware" style software in the marketplace over the past couple of years and whilst it remains useful for some smaller businesses (and maybe even you) it's usually easier if your payroll software completes these tasks.

The reality is that it's now more likely in an environment where many of the payroll software solutions have decent functionality which means middleware is often not required.

Middleware is used far less and even some of our larger clients who had to use middleware are now looking at integrated payroll software solutions. After all if you're a business of any size why would you pay for two pieces of software when actually one will do the job?

Therefore before you pay for any form of 'Middleware' solution it's important to check your payroll software to ensure that you're just not duplicating functionality already provided (or has the potential to be provided) through your payroll software.

However if there's a bunch of gaps in your payroll software, you're not too keen on changing the system you use and you want to automate and systemise the auto enrolment process it might be worth considering whether 'middleware' software will make your life easier.

Understanding the limitations of payroll

Having payroll software which helps out with much of the 'heavy lifting' required to comply with automatic enrolment on a regular basis, or knowing what the gaps in the payroll processes are so you can complete them manually, is an important part of ongoing journey of complying with automatic enrolment.

However if you're relying on your payroll software to do all the tasks required so that you meet all your auto enrolment obligations you're likely to miss out on completing some of the important tasks you need to do in order to fully comply.

If we go back to our 'three circles' of auto enrolment you'll remember there are three overlapping circles to consider...

Pensions, Payroll & Regulation.

As we've already discussed when we were talking about the 'circle of regulation' there are obligations you need to meet which your payroll software will do.

However many of your obligations as an employer, even with the most sophisticated payroll software currently available on the market, will need to be done manually without the use of your payroll.
The best way to understand these gaps is step by step...

First understand the obligations your business has under the regulation.

Thirdly understand what your pension provider can do to fill these regulatory gaps and choose an alternative pension provider if required.

Secondly understand what your payroll software does to help fill these regulatory gaps and make a decision to keep your existing software or not.

You'll be left with a number of gaps you need to fill where you'll need either a manual process (or support software) to help you do this.

This gives you an insight into what you need to complete manually within your business in order to comply you can then build systems within your business to get these 'tasks' completed on an ongoing basis.

As you can see by now, automatic enrolment is a relatively complicated business. It will take a decent amount of time to prepare for the obligations and will potentially mean you'll need to make changes to a number of elements of your business.

If you're currently reading this and feel a bit overwhelmed, you're not alone.

However complying with automatic enrolment can and has been done by employers without external help or support at all.

If you feel, even after reading this book, that you need additional help and support to both guide you through the automatic enrolment process and to ensure you continue to comply I completely understand…

This next chapter is just for you.…

Chapter 7

Help and support

Before we start this chapter in earnest and due to the fact that together we've got this far through the maze of auto enrolment I just wanted to say one thing….

Well done!

If you're like most people, and as you've probably seen by now, automatic enrolment legislation is a tiny bit more complicated than you probably realised when you first picked this particular publication up.

So it's worth saying at this stage that you've already done brilliantly to take the time reading this book to ensure you fully understand the practical issues you need to think about to ensure your business complies.

By now having taken the time to read this book you should be in a position where having understood your obligations, navigated the "Circles of Automatic Enrolment" and considered the decisions you need to make one decision before all others…

Do I need extra help to ensure my business complies with automatic enrolment regulation or not?

It may be the case that having read this book, studied the pension regulators detailed guidance and taken the time to see how this applies to your business you might be completely ready to comply satisfactorily without any support.

'Doing it yourself' might be absolutely right for your business and for a number of companies across the UK they'll be busy complying without the support of any external professionals or additional support solutions.

However before you make a definitive decision on whether to get extra help or not there's are a few factors worth considering first..

Money vs Time

In many small businesses time is at a premium. Most of us are busy running our businesses with a focus on the particular profession or trade which earns us a living.

As you'll understand by now complying with automatic enrolment if you decide to 'do it yourself' will potentially take one main resource.

This resource is time.

The reality is that every employer in the land who decides not to seek any support to comply with automatic enrolment will need to assign a chunk of time within their businesses (either the business owners time or one of their employees) to ensure the business complies.

Therefore if you're running a business, or are responsible for automatic enrolment in your particular business the question you need to ask is relatively straightforward...

Is it worth paying for professional support due to the time it'll free up for me and my team to work on and in our business?

The amount of time you'll be spending complying with automatic enrolment will depend on the nature of your business, the complexity of your workforce and the skills and experience of the individual it's assigned to.

However for your business it might be worth considering seeking support in order to ensure you and your team can continue to focus on what you do best.

Practical experience

For most small businesses complying with automatic enrolment legislation is brand new. It's therefore fair to say that most small employers have little or no experience complying with the legislation.

Therefore one of the main reasons for seeking help, guidance and support through the automatic enrolment process is that many automatic enrolment professionals have bucket loads of practical experience in already successfully helping employers comply.

This isn't to say that small employers can't comply successfully on their own. Many employers will successfully comply with automatic enrolment without any external support at all.

However for many employers having access to an individual (or a service) which takes the practical knowledge of past experience so that their journey to automatic enrolment compliance far smoother makes sense.

Working with a professional or support service with previous experience of working with employers has a couple of clear tangible benefits…

Firstly practical experience provides knowledge of what previous employers have done right (and sometimes more importantly wrong) when complying with automatic enrolment.

For you having access to a service containing individuals with this practical experience can be invaluable because they'll share this knowledge which could make your businesses journey to automatic enrolment far smoother.

Secondly, most professionals have spent a decent amount of time on the phone to the pensions regulator (I know I have!) and have clarified certain elements of the regulation.

Having access to a support service containing professionals who have spent time clarifying certain aspects of the regulation should allow you to gain access to this level of clarification and could potentially avoid you spending too much time on the phone to the pensions regulator having to clarify certain points relating to your business.

However for any of this to be relevant you need to work with a professional (or support service) with decent practical experience in helping employers comply with automatic enrolment.

Therefore if you're considering working with a professional or support service so that you've got access to their practical experience it's worth asking them some questions around the level of practical experience they've had (I've talked about some of the questions you might want to ask on page 38)

Filling the gaps

When it comes to complying with automatic enrolment regulation different businesses have different challenges, different areas of strength and different resources within their business.

This means that it's likely that employers will be comfortable with some aspects of the rules but not with others.

For example employers we've worked with were completely comfortable with complying with the regulation but not with the payroll or pensions element of automatic enrolment compliance.

Others were happy with all elements of complying with the rules but struggled with selecting the right pension for their employees.

Therefore many employers will choose to comply with automatic enrolment within their own business but 'fill the gaps' in the areas they feel less comfortable with by getting additional support.

This might mean complying directly with the regulation but using a professional or support service to manage payroll and select a pension on their behalf.

It might mean complying with the regulation up to their staging date but using a support service to keep up to date with any future changes.

It might mean dealing with the 'circles of payroll' and the 'circles of pension' internally but getting additional support to comply with your regulatory responsibilities.

What's right for you and your business depends on a number of factors and the best judge of that will be you.

However it's worth considering doing what you can do within your business to comply with the automatic enrolment obligations and then seeking professional advice or a support service to 'fill the gaps'.

What support is available

Now we've talked through the reasons why you might want to get some extra help complying with automatic enrolment let's explore the wide range of options you've got when seeking help.

First we're going to explore the free support available for you and your business. This will include the support you can get from the pensions regulator, potential support from your current or new pension provider and free guidance you can find online.

We're then going to explore the range of support available on a consultancy basis. This will include all of the professionals we've seen actively engaged in this space including financial advisers and planners, accountants and payroll bureaus.

Then we'll talk about the systemised support available. This'll include task management services, payroll software and software provided through 'middleware' software solutions.

Free Support

The pensions regulator

The government organisation responsible for notifying employers of their obligations under the new rules, encouraging employers to act sooner rather than later, applying penalties to employers who don't comply in time and provide support for employers who need help and support is called "The pensions regulator".

As you'd expect from the body set up by government to be responsible for the successful implementation of automatic enrolment they also provide a massively comprehensive resource, both through their website and by providing guidance over the phone all at no cost.

If you're an employer who's approaching their staging date one of the first ports of call you should make is to the pension regulators website to help you get your head around the new regulation, help understand how legislation specifically applies to your business and to make use of some of the really useful tools available at no cost through the regulator[24].

It's worth highlighting some of the particularly useful tools for employers on the pensions regulator website which help you with

---

[24] For the best place to start look here
http://www.thepensionsregulator.gov.uk/employers.aspx

the different elements of automatic enrolment law…[25]
This page links to the step by step guide provided through the
regulator to automatic enrolment compliance.

The guide highlights the pertinent points you need to be aware of
to comply with automatic enrolment regulation, many of which
you've read about in this book, and points to additional resources
on the pension regulators website which helps clarify certain
aspects of how automatic enrolment applies to your business.

In addition to the interactive guide there's a number of really useful
tools designed to ensure that you can work through certain aspects
of the regulation.

In addition to the interactive guide a useful tool is the ability to
create an "action plan" for your business online.[26]:-

All you'll need to do is put in your staging date and this tool will
provide a framework for you to follow to complete your journey
towards automatic enrolment compliance.

It's important to be clear about one thing relating to this tool.
Whilst the tool will provide an overview of the aspects of your
automatic enrolment project you need to consider it doesn't break
down the small tasks you need to complete on the tool itself.

To do this you'll need to 'click through' and follow the more
detailed written guides in order to ensure you're completing all of
the more specific tasks to ensure you comply.

---

[25] You can find useful tools here
http://www.thepensionsregulator.gov.uk/employers/your-step-by-step-guide-to-automatic-enrolment.aspx
[26] You can find the action plan tool here
http://www.thepensionsregulator.gov.uk/employers/planning-for-automatic-enrolment.aspx

Also, it's important to remember that whilst you can use the tool as and when you need to, it's not a dynamic tool as currently it doesn't contact you with reminders of when tasks need to be completed.

However if you're an employer who has a decent amount of time resource within their business and is looking for a free tool which supports their journey but without some of the beneficial commercial tools available in the marketplace then the pensions regulators website is a worthwhile starting point.

In addition to the website which provides massively useful and detailed guidance there's also additional support.

You can call the regulator to clarify certain aspects of the legislation (currently the best number to call is 0845 600 1011) together with the opportunity to email queries to the regulator or, if you're really traditional, you can write a good old fashioned letter to the regulator.

Currently the best email address to contact the regulator is customersupport@autoenrol.tpr.gov.uk

If you've decided you wanted to write to the regulator here's the best current address:-

The Pensions Regulator,
PO Box 16314,
Birmingham,
B23 3JP.

It's also worth mentioning that as the pensions regulator has the regulatory responsible for automatic enrolment their website will be an up to date and definitive resource. This is the reason their site will be somewhere worth checking in on regularly not only to ensure you reach your staging date compliantly but are also up to speed with changes in automatic enrolment regulation.

Read all about it

Over the past year or so more, and especially since smaller businesses have had to comply, there has been plenty written about automatic enrolment.

Therefore by searching for automatic enrolment related topics in the news it's probably you'll find an article which might be useful when you're planning and preparing to comply with automatic enrolment.

However for definitive information, support and advice I'd suggest that instead of relying on the press it's worth visiting the pensions regulator website directly.

On the web

There's plenty of free resources explaining and discussing a wide range of particular aspects of automatic enrolment on the internet.

First there's a bunch of really good people writing decent amount of free content which you can access for free on the web.
It'll take you some time to separate the wheat from the chaff, the good from the bad (and the sometimes ugly) but there's some great content out there for free for those who are looking for it.

Also it's worth seeing who the key individuals are in the automatic enrolment marketplace to see what they've got to say and, if you're a social media user, perhaps connect with them on Twitter and Linkedin.

As a starting point you're more than welcome to follow me on Twitter (You can find me @ChrisDaems) as well as @AEinabox so that you'll get access to the insights we share on the world of automatic enrolment.

However when we're talking about the automatic enrolment knowledge you pick up from the web let me express one slight word of caution…

Whilst there's loads of great content on t'internet on a wide range of financial subjects, including how businesses comply with automatic enrolment, there's also a decent amount which (and I'm being polite here) isn't particular useful.

Therefore if you're using free web based resources be careful to validate the information you're getting with a couple of alternative sources.

Support from your selected pension provider

One of the other routes to free guidance and support is through either your existing pension provider or the provider you've selected to be the right people to provide a pension so that you can comply with automatic enrolment.

Currently the information and support each pension provider gives you access to is mixed to be best. Some providers offer fantastically high levels of support and others none at all.

Also it's likely that the support you'll get from the pension provider is only available if you're already a client of their or alternatively using them for a new scheme you intend to set up.

One important thing to bear in mind when it comes to getting support from your pension provider is this isn't the only factor you should consider when selecting the right home for you and your employees money.
For more information on the other important factors you should consider when selecting an appropriate pension scheme for you, your employees and your business it's worth revisiting Chapter 5.

Consultancy support

There's a decent number of professionals, with specialisms in different areas, who should be able to help you with automatic enrolment.

However before we explore the different professionals who can help you it's worth remembering something important...

All professions (including accountancy, financial advice and payroll) tend to be pretty broad churches. This means that some involved in these particular professions might have a decent amount of expertise in helping employers comply with automatic enrolment regulation whilst others might have none at all.

I've used some generalisations in this section based on my experience. However it's always important if you're choosing to work with a professional of any kind to ask a bunch of questions to ensure that they've got relevant experience, knowledge and expertise to help you through the automatic enrolment minefield.

In this section I'm going to detail who the main consultants are, where and how they might be able to help and where they may be able to "fill the gaps" in the automatic enrolment project within your own business...

Employee benefits consultants

Traditionally a lot of the larger businesses who complied with automatic enrolment used Employee Benefits Consultants to ensure they complied with the automatic enrolment process.

Whilst there are still a few active employee benefit consultancy businesses involved in helping small and medium sized employers very often their consultancy fees mean that this option is prohibitively expensive for many smaller businesses.

Employee benefits consultants tend to have a decent amount of expertise in helping larger employers put in place a suite of employee benefits and this traditionally included the pension.

Therefore traditionally employee benefits consultants have a decent amount of pension expertise but also their experience of working with larger businesses mean they'll understand quite a lot about internal systems and processes within businesses.

However the nature of their businesses means that their experience will be more often in helping larger employers than smaller ones.

Financial Advisers and Financial Planners

Whilst many financial advisers and planners have decided to focus on the more conventional private client work (working with individuals managing their wealth) as opposed to helping SME employers with their automatic enrolment obligations there are still quite a few who specialise in this area of work.

Many financial advisers and planners core area of strength when it comes to automatic enrolment and as you'd expect is in the research and recommendation of an appropriate pension scheme for your business.

Also financial advisers and planners tend to be pretty good at understanding the complexities of automatic enrolment law in a pretty robust way (if they've decided to specialise in this particular area) with many having already taken the pensions management institute qualification.

However many financial planners and advisers won't have dealt with the intricacies of payroll in the past and for many this might be an area you'll have to get additional extra support perhaps from your accountant, payroll bureau or an external support solution.

It's important if you decide to work with a financial planner in this area that you select one who has relevant experience and expertise in this market and I've already talked about some of the questions you can ask your financial planner or adviser to ensure they are the right person for you to work with (you can find these in Chapter 2).

Accountants

Your accountant is for many of you a natural place to initially seek support and guidance with the automatic enrolment process.

Typically accountants are really good at managing the payroll obligations under automatic enrolment with many accountants managing payroll on behalf of their clients already.

Also, accountants by the nature of their business tend to be pretty good and understanding and complying with regulation.

Even though for many accountants automatic enrolment regulation might be relatively new our experience is that most accountants have taken the time to understand the regulation really well.

However where accountants might have a gap in their expertise is in the process of selecting an appropriate pension. In our experience different accountants are managing this in different ways.

Many are partnering up with financial advice and planning firms to provide advice to both their existing and prospective clients in order to fill the pension advice gap.

Others are leaving the choice of pension selection to employers.

There are accountants however who are partnering up with an individual or a panel or particular pension provider(s).

A word of warning if your accountant is taking this particular approach and you're happy as an employer to go with whatever pension scheme your accountant recommends.

It is down to the employer to select an appropriate pension scheme on behalf of their employees.

Whilst allowing your accountant to select a particular scheme on behalf of you makes sense in terms of removing hassle and efficiency you still need to make sure that your accountant on your behalf has done a decent amount of due diligence to select the right provider or panel of providers.

Payroll Bureaus

As you'd expect your payroll bureau are normally really good at running payroll!

It's fair to say that if you want an expert in payroll, and in our experience this includes the automatic enrolment obligations which sit in payroll, a bureau will have more practical experience than any other professional.

Also, by the nature of their business, payroll bureaus are generally excellent at managing systems and putting processes in place in order to solve process related issues regarding automatic enrolment.

In our experience payroll bureaus, like many of the other professionals involved in the automatic enrolment market, have areas where they feel less comfortable helping with.

In our experience the area that many payroll bureaus feel less comfortable with is guiding employers in the 'circle of pensions'.

Therefore if you're aiming for support from your payroll bureau you may need additional support to select an appropriate pension scheme for your business and your employees.

There are a few payroll bureaus who are deciding to partner with one pension provider based on how compatible the pension scheme is with the systems they use.

However, and for fear of repeating myself, it's important to show as an employer you've gone through a process where you've made a decision about selecting an appropriate pension scheme for you and your employers not only based on its ease of use for your payroll bureau but is the best scheme for you and your employers.

When it comes to complying with the processes within the 'circle of regulation' payroll bureaus tend to take two clear approaches.

Either they offer their clients are fully serviced solution which includes helping employers with many of their obligations under the 'circle of regulation'.

Other payroll bureaus want to specialise in helping employers specifically with the payroll obligations of automatic enrolment and either work with fellow professionals with expertise in other areas of the automatic enrolment or make it clear to employers that they need to meet an employer's obligations under the 'circle of regulation' themselves.

Either way is fine. However as an employer it's important to be clear what your payroll bureau will do for you, and what they won't do for you.

Automatic enrolment consultants

Over the past 18 months or so there have been a decent number of automatic enrolment consultancy businesses popping up.

These businesses are run by individuals with a wide and diverse range of experience and qualification from having worked in larger businesses having helped them comply to having been HR consultants who have expanded their services into the automatic enrolment arena.

In our experience these automatic enrolment consultants are really good at understanding the regulation and how to help businesses comply with the regulation.

Their level of expertise in the 'pensions' and 'payroll' elements of automatic enrolment often depends on the background of the consultant you work with.

Therefore it's worth again asking sufficient questions to both understand how an automatic enrolment consultant will help you and where you'll need to get further support to ensure you comply compliantly.

Other consultancy support

There's also a number of other professionals who can help you with certain aspects of automatic enrolment.

Employment and contract lawyers are best placed to check your existing employment contracts to confirm whether changes need to be made or not.

Specific individuals with project management might work with you to ensure you've got the systems and processes within your businesses (although this was far more common in larger businesses than smaller ones)

What software support is available?

In the run up to auto enrolment legislation being intruded and for the first year or so the software available was designed primarily to help larger employers comply.

However as the impact of automatic enrolment has grown and continues to grow in scope and scale and with an estimated 1.8

million employers having to comply in the next couple of years the software market has continued to mature to reflect this changing market.

This is for a couple of reasons…

Firstly, as the employers who now need to comply are significantly smaller, they are typically looking for ways to get help and guidance through the automatic enrolment process at a far lower cost than typical face to face consultation support.

Secondly, as employers had to comply, lessons were learnt by the employers, the consultants and the software providers in the aspects of the automatic enrolment process employers specifically needed help and support in.

Therefore we've seen a bunch of different software solutions emerge each providing different levels of support depending on what employers are looking for.

So, let's start by exploring the software which can support you and your business through the automatic enrolment process with the software currently being provided by...

Payroll software providers

There are many payroll software providers who have built, developed and are now distributing additional 'plugins' to their existing software which are designed to help businesses comply with automatic enrolment.

These plugins typically automate many of the 'payroll' tasks required of your business when complying with automatic enrolment.

I've detailed the particular tasks the typical 'automatic enrolment ready' payroll software should and can complete in Chapter 6 however they usually include calculating contributions, working out who needs to be enrolled into the scheme and on occasion issuing the regulatory communications all employers are required to distribute.

However the payroll software market as I write this remains a particularly diverse one. Some payroll software has all the functionality detailed in Chapter 6, some have none and some have some features but are far from fully functional.

It's therefore important to check with your provider what your payroll software does and more importantly what functionality it doesn't have.

Also, it's important to remember that using a payroll software 'plugin' to support some of the tasks you need to complete to help you comply doesn't mean that all of your tasks are automatically completed.

Whilst payroll software can make many of the ongoing tasks within payroll a lot easier it doesn't complete many of the tasks required of you as an employer, may not keep you updated in changes in legislation and it's highly unlikely to help you perform such tasks as nominating a contact on your behalf or registering your business with the regulator.

The other factor to consider when considering using a payroll plugin to perform a lot of the tasks in an automated way is cost.

Whilst much of the payroll software is costed competitively and tends to compare favourably to either manually completing the payroll related tasks it's worth considering cost and if you're prepared to make the change shopping around for a payroll software provider which both gives you the functionality you need and provides great value for money.

Project management, task management & compliance tool

There's also a number of software tools designed to assist you and your business to comply. They will not only help you with complying with the regulation but also helps you with managing your automatic enrolment project.

A number of tools exist in this market including AE in a Box, the software tool I helped (along with my brilliant team) develop but there are a number of alternatives including AE Wizard, AME (provided from Aviva) and EnrolSME.

This market is continuously expanding and growing with each piece of software providing different functionality.

However before you do this, let me answer a question which if you're like many people will be at the forefront of your mind right now...

What does an automatic enrolment compliance tool do and why might I want to use one?

Many employers when complying with automatic enrolment feel like they need additional help and support when complying with automatic enrolment regulation.

However many relatively small employers, businesses who need to comply between 2015 and 2018 and probably including your own organisation, have a couple of additional issues which didn't occur as often in larger businesses.

Firstly many small businesses don't either have the cash, or alternatively the willingness to spend loads of cash, on getting a professional in to help them comply with the automatic enrolment process.

Secondly, although smaller businesses might not have the capacity or willingness to pay consultancy feeds many small businesses still

Three Circles – The practical guide to Automatic Enrolment

need support and guidance to help them complete the tasks required to comply with automatic enrolment and ensure they comply on an ongoing basis.

These two issues create a gap. A gap where small businesses need support but where having a professional to help guide them through the intricacies of the automatic enrolment process unaffordable.

This gap is increasingly being filled by employers by the aforementioned software based compliance.

These tools are designed to help employers comply with automatic enrolment by providing a wide range of support by providing supporting in the following areas…

Creates a project plan for the employer

For most businesses, including perhaps yours, complying with automatic enrolment starts with a project plan.

As an employer there's nothing stopping you building and creating your own plan and creating your own project in order to comply with automatic enrolment. In fact chapter 3 and appendix I in this book will give you the guidance you need to do the job.

However if you feel you need help to do this many of the automatic enrolment project management tools, AE in a Box included, make this process really straightforward.

By sharing some pertinent information about your business many of the project management tools available in the marketplace builds your project plan, sets appropriate timelines and immediately inserts all of the tasks you need to complete to comply with the regulation.

However for many employers the process of building the project plan is the 'easy bit'.

The challenge comes when they try to make automatic enrolment compliance easy by breaking it's component parts down into small actionable tasks in order to make the project actionable.

This is why so many employers find the following functionality provided by these tools so useful…

Simplifying auto enrolment tasks by breaking the project down into bite size chunks.

The reality of automatic enrolment is that there's a decent amount to do in order for you and your business to comply successfully.

However the fact that there is a lot for employers to do up to their staging date is that this can be overwhelming.

That's why in addition to building the project plan designed to help the employer structure their automatic enrolment plan these systems are designed to help employers break the automatic enrolment project down into bite size chunks for employers to follow.

This means that employers have an already built project plan broken down into bite size chunks an employer can easily follow.

Therefore having a support system build a project plan and break this project down into bite size chunks makes the process of complying with automatic enrolment far easier which is why automatic enrolment project management tools continue to grow in popularity.

However how can employers efficiently keep track of the tasks that have been completed, what's left to complete and who's completed specific tasks…

That's why many employers find the next tool usually contained within these type of systems really helpful…

Keeps track of automatic enrolment tasks together with creating an audit trail of tasks.

Many of these project management tools keep track of the tasks you need to comply, the tasks yet to be completed, overdue tasks and contact you to let you know the next steps in your automatic enrolment project.

In addition to this many of these project management tools provide an audit trail highlighting who completed specific tasks within your business and when they've completed these jobs.

However for many of the employers using these project management tools they are still working in conjunction with a professional so that the particular professional can provide support when required.

That's why many of these systems allow…

Professional access so you can use the tool with your accountant / financial adviser

Whilst many of these tools are designed so that they can be used independently without a professional many employers like the idea of having support as and when required from the professionals they work with.

Therefore many of these project management tools allow employers to work in conjunction with the professionals who help them so that they can provide additional support over and above the platform when required.

However sometimes users of these platforms want answers to technical questions directly.

That's why a lot of these platforms…

Provide access to experts designed to answer queries.

Many of these support solutions allow access, usually via an online support service, to professionals who can help with specific queries.

However many of the challenges employers are currently facing and will face in the coming years have already been faced by employers who are in the process of compliance or have already complied.

This is why many of these project management tools…

Provide access to a range of fully searchable frequently asked questions.

The automatic enrolment support tools usually have a bunch of frequently asked questions with many of these tools being frequently updated as and when new queries get asked and answered.

This means that if you're using an automatic enrolment support platform you get access to answers to questions from a knowledge base which has been built using the experience of both the builders of the platform as well as its users.

However many employers find that the greatest challenge when it comes to automatic enrolment is being able to select a pension which is right for their business.

Therefore many of these support platforms include the ability to…
Help employers decide whether their current pension scheme can be used and if not helps them select and apply for a new scheme.

With many of the employers approaching automatic enrolment

needing to go through the process of checking whether their existing pension scheme can be used and if not having to select a new pension many of the automatic enrolment support solutions make this process easy.

At AE in a Box we've conducted a bunch of due diligence to filter down the pension selection choice so that users have a choice of three high quality schemes to select from.

However other support systems have a different process with some systems allowing choice from all of the pensions on the market and other support solutions providing only one choice.

Regardless of support solution you decide to use (if you decide to use one) there should be functionality within this support solution which makes pension selection easier.

However once a pensions been selected it's time to work out whether the employers payroll system is appropriate. So many of the automatic enrolment platforms provide...

Help for employers so that they can decide whether their current payroll system is suitable.

Whilst deciding to keep using their existing payroll software or bureau, changing to a more efficient alternative or using 'middleware' to fill some of these gaps in the 'circle of payroll' many of the support solutions provide support for employers guiding them through a decision making process.

These automatic enrolment support solutions guide employers through a thought process which help identify if their current payroll software is fit for purpose and the options employers have if they don't.

However as we've talked about throughout this book employers need to continue to comply with automatic enrolment regulation and keep on top of any changes in regulation as well as their ongoing obligations. Some of these support solutions help do this by…

Provide constant updates as automatic enrolment compliance continues to change, keeping employers updated of these changes and the ongoing tasks they need to complete.

The reality of automatic enrolment is that for an employer reaching their staging date compliantly is the start, and definitely not the end, of their automatic enrolment obligations.

Some of these support services therefore provide you with constant updates to confirm you continue to ensure that your business complies. They do this by keeping you updated as and when regulation changes.

However it's also important to remember that some of the tools available in this marketplace don't provide any ongoing support but instead are only designed to ensure you comply up to your staging date.

Ultimately the judgement on whether to select a support service with ongoing support or not is up to you.

However in our experience it's worth having access to the additional support beyond your staging date so that you're fully informed of changes in regulation and so you've got a point of contact in the future.

Now we've fully explored the features most automatic enrolment support solutions, including AE in a Box, provides to support employers it's now time to move onto the next type of software support designed to help you with your automatic enrolment obligations.

Middleware

In the early days of automatic enrolment "middleware" played a significant role in supporting many large and medium sized employers perform many of the functions required in order to comply.

However as payroll software becomes more sophisticated and has started to include many of the features of middleware software there's now less of a marketplace for independent middleware software.

However if you're finding that your payroll software doesn't perform all the functions required to help you and your business with automatic enrolment sufficiently but for whatever reason you don't want to switch your payroll software to a more comprehensive alternative it might be worth considering how middleware can help fill this gap.

Chapter 8

Taking action and the next steps

So far in this book we've talked about what automatic enrolment is and it's monumental impact.

We've talked about what you need to do to create your automatic enrolment plan as well as deep diving into the three circles which should have helped you make sense of the tasks you need to complete to practically comply with automatic enrolment legislation.

First we looked at the first 'circle' of automatic enrolment, regulation and detailed the tasks you need to complete and the things you need to consider in order to comply, the decisions you need to make prior to your staging date and the decisions you need to make relating to picking appropriate contribution levels and potentially postponing when you automatically enrol your employees.

Then we considered the second 'circle' of automatic enrolment – pensions. We talked about some of the decisions you need to make both when it comes to considering your existing scheme (if you have one) and what to consider when putting a new scheme in place if you need to.

Then we discussed the third circle of automatic enrolment – payroll. In this chapter we looked at the decisions you need to make when looking at your payroll software so that you can make some of these ongoing obligations as pain free as possible and considered whether using 'middleware' or performing some of these tasks manually was a more appropriate approach.

Then we looked at the help and support you and employers like you can receive to ensure you navigate the automatic enrolment maze successfully.

From the support you can access which doesn't cost you a penny all the way through to bespoke consultancy services provided by a range of professionals across the UK.

In addition to this we talked about the software support provided from payroll software through to automatic enrolment support solutions through to 'middleware' and thoroughly explored how these support solutions can help your business.

It's fair to say we've explored the landscape of automatic enrolment pretty thoroughly and by now you should have your plan in place, understand what you need to do from a practical perspective and have an idea of, if any, what support you need as well as what support is available.

So now you've got a thorough understanding of the automatic enrolment landscape and the practical steps you need to take to comply there's only one thing left to do…

Take action!

However before you start taking action let me stop and share with you a little tip about ensuring you're keeping track of the action you take...

Creating and keeping an audit trail

One thing it's important to do is have a system which allows you to track when tasks are being completed and by whom.

Having this audit trail in place is important due to the fact that you want to make sure that you can evidence when, how and who completed these tasks within your business.

This can be tracked using a spreadsheet, using a business's internal audit systems or one of the automatic enrolment support tools I mentioned in the previous chapter.

Also, if you're working with a professional it's important to be clear about who is keeping this 'audit trail'.

Therefore if you've chosen to work with a professional it's important to confirm with the professional you're working with who's retaining this information, and if it's the professional who's looking after this data where it's being stored.

So once you've taken the action to ensure you comply up to your staging date you're all done right?

Well, erm, No.

You now need to know what you need to do to comply on an ongoing basis…

How to comply on an ongoing basis with automatic enrolment legislation

So, let's explore the ongoing tasks you need to perform on an ongoing basis to ensure that your business continues to meet its obligations under the automatic enrolment rules...

Payroll processes

Under automatic enrolment regulation you need to do a number of things to ensure you continue to comply each and every time you process your payroll.

If you're using payroll software with built in automatic enrolment functionality much of this work should be automated by the software you use

However, and as we've talked about already, it's worth checking the tasks you need to complete on a regular basis are completed automatically as part of your payroll service (you can read about the questions you need to ask your payroll software provider in chapter 6).

These ongoing tasks include opting individuals into a workplace pension if they start to earn over a specific amount, communicate the fact that they're going to be opted in, calculate pension contributions and make the pension payments to the pension provider.

Process opt-ins and opt outs

If you've got an employee at any stage who decides to opt in early or you've got an employee who wants to opt out you need as an employer to support them to do this.

It's also important that you keep records of these opt in and opt outs and maintain these records of any time your employee decides to either go into or come out of the pension scheme.

Decide whether you're going to continue with your current level of certification, or not, every 18 months.

You can decide to change the way you calculate your pension contributions into a pension scheme every 18 months. We cover what you need to do and how to do this on page (83) and you can find more information on this particular point in the pensions regulators detailed guidance here[27]:-

Re-enrol employees in every three years.

Every three years you need to re-enrol all of your employees who have opted out. This means that if you've had employees who have chosen to opt out need to be opted back in (if they are entitled workers) every three years.

Now at this stage it's worth making an important point…

The 'opt back in' date is always three years from the staging date of the employer (and then every three years on an ongoing basis) as opposed to three years after the staging date of each employee.

Let's explain this particular point with a practical example…

Bamons Ltd staging date is on the 1st September 2015 and employs 12 people.

Over the course of the next year and a half 4 of those 12 people opt out of the pension scheme.

On the 1st September 2018 all of those employees need to be re-enrolled into a scheme.

Therefore one of the regular tasks you need to complete, every three years after your staging date, is re-enrol everyone who's opted out.

Administer refunds (if required)

If someone decides to opt out and you need to pay them a refund (we've talked about the detail on this in page 95) you need to make sure this is done in a timely and efficient manner.

---

[27] www.thepensionsregulator.gov.uk/docs/detailed-guidance-4.pdf

Increase contributions when appropriate

As we've discussed contributions are due to increase at periodic dates over the course of the next few years (we've talked about this specifically on page 84).

It's therefore important that you and your business schedules these increases in contribution levels so that you can ensure you're both communicating to your workforce that their contribution levels are due to increase together with increasing their contributions.

Keep up to date in changes in regulation

The reality is that when compared to countries who have had similar regimes to automatic enrolment for decades, the regulation in the UK are still in their infancy.

However if you consider some of the countries where similar systems are in place the regulation continues to adapt and change.

If, for example, you consider Australia, where their version of automatic enrolment (Superannuation) has been established for a number of years you'll see that there are regular and consistent changes to the rules.

Therefore it's important to ensure you have a system in place designed to keep you up to date with the potentially constant and consistent changes to the rules you need to comply with.

You can do this in one of three ways...

Firstly as by this stage you should have registered with the regulator you should receive ongoing and consistent communication from the regulator about any upcoming changes and how to cope with these changes.

However it's important to remember that in order for this approach to be successful for you and your business you need to ensure that you take the time to fully understand the letters and emails you receive from the regulator and turn this information about any potential changes into actionable 'tasks' within your business.

Secondly if you're working with a professional and have an ongoing commercial relationship it's important to ensure part of this relationship you've got with your adviser is that they keep you informed of any changes in the rules you need to take action on.

And thirdly if you've decided to use an automatic enrolment support service which keeps you informed for the longer term. These systems will keep you informed of any changes you need to make and create 'tasks' designed for you to make the amendments required. However it's important to check that the support service you use does promise to provide this task.

So, now you know what you need to do consistently with some tasks needing to be completed at each and every payroll period and others not needing to be completed every 3 years.

As we've mentioned we don't know when and whether certain elements of the regulation will change, and in fact whether they will at all.

However it's important for you to keep your 'ear to the ground' either by using an ongoing automatic enrolment service or by opting in and taking action on what the regulator communicates directly.

By now you've got everything you need to comply with automatic enrolment legislation. There's only one thing left to say…

There are parts of the automatic enrolment process which are pretty complex. However if you take your time to understand automatic enrolment, plan well and then take action compliance is achievable.

Good luck!

Addendum i

Example Auto Enrolment Plan

Staging Date and Timeline

- Our PAYE Reference number is 123/AB456. This means our staging date is the 1st August 2017.
- We currently have 10 employees.
- We intend to start preparing for automatic enrolment at the start of March 2017 so we have 5 months to prepare.

Responsibility and contingency

- Within our business Susan Terry (the office manager) is going to be responsible for automatic enrolment and will be registered as our primary contact.
- Susan is away on annual leave September the 12th 2015 until the 4th of January 2016. Therefore we need to ensure that any tasks due within this period are completed by Lee Paul.
- In the event of Susan being unable to manage and complete all tasks required to ensure we comply with automatic enrolment Lee Paul will be responsible for completing these tasks. This contingency will occur if Susan Terry is off for longer than 2 weeks if previously unplanned (i.e. sickness or leaving the business).

- We will be using AE in a Box to track all tasks and ensure that all tasks are completed within appropriate timescales as well as creating an audit trail to confirm when and who completed specific tasks.

Understand automatic enrolment

To fully ensure we understand our obligations under automatic enrolment we will be doing the following:-

- We will conduct research on the pension regulators website.
- We will seek help and support from our accountant.
- We will use the resources available via AE in a Box. Both Susan Terry and Lee Paul will be tasked within our business to understand automatic enrolment and ensure they have the knowledge and resources required to meet our obligations under the regulation.

Support

- We have decided to use AE in a Box's Pension Selector Tool to help us with the pension selection process.
- Our payroll is currently managed via our accountant (AB Smith + Co.). We will continue running our payroll through our accountant with the accountant managing the payroll functionality of our automatic enrolment process. Our accountant intends to charge us an additional £30 + vat per month for this service.

- We intend to use AE in a Box to ensure we are up to date with our regulatory obligations, ensure we're consistently updated with regulatory change and provide technical support. We pay £29 + vat per month to use AE in a Box.

Circle of Regulation

- We are not going to be bringing our staging date forward as we feel we want to spend the current time available up until our staging date focusing on complying and therefore didn't want to add any additional pressure to this process.
- Susan Terry will be our nominated primary point of contact. Our secondary point of contact is our Accountant, AB Smith + Co.
- Having done an initial assessment we know that currently we have 7 eligible jobholders who will be automatically enrolled into the pension and 3 entitled workers who will not be automatically enrolled however we know they can join the scheme if they wish but they will not receive any employer contributions.
- Lee Paul will be looking into the current employment contracts that we have and see if there are any discrepancy's when it comes to allowing people into a pension's scheme and confirm the notice period in the contracts.
- Susan Terry will be raising awareness of automatic enrolment by sending everyone emails through their work addresses. We will also be getting a financial planning to come in and explain the new rules to employees.
- Our current payroll software is Payroll 987, we need to check whether they it calculates contributions on our behalf and if not then we need to decide whether to use middleware or not.

- We intend to use the maximum deferral period (3 months) this will apply to all existing employees from staging date as well as new starters.
- All opt ins/early opt in requests should be emailed to Susan Terry who will then opt them in using our payroll software.
- For opt outs, employees need to email Susan Terry who will give employees a template letter they need to complete and give back to Susan who will then process through payroll and notify the pension provider.
- We will be communicating with the team through email. It will be the responsibility of Susan Terry and if she is not in then it will be Lee Paul's responsibility.
- Susan Terry is responsible for registering with the regulator as well as apply for the Government Gateway.

We have chosen to use AE in a Box which lets us know when we need to increase our minimum contribution levels.

1. Office Server as well as retaining opt out letters and opt in emails and additional non payroll documentation
2. Cloud based storage solution

- As we are going to be using AE in a Box they update the system with any changes in regulation and produce tasks for us to complete to reflect this. We have also signed up for the monthly update emails from The Pensions Regulator which will inform us of any updates/changes that they are making.

Circle of Pensions

- We do not have an existing pension
- We are going to be using AE in a Box's Pension Selector tool to pick our pension

- Factors that are important to us and employees when selecting a pension scheme are:-

1. Financial Strength
2. Costs
3. Fund choices
4. Good level of service
5. Compatible with our payroll

- We are going to talk with our employees regarding a pension scheme and take into account their comments. Susan Terry will be responsible for the pension selection after speaking to the Directors of the business.
- Susan Terry is responsible for the pension application process

---

Circle of Payroll

- Susan Terry is going to be responsible for checking that our payroll software is fit for purpose with the help of AE in a Box
- Our payroll software is fit for purpose therefore payroll will be able to complete specific payroll related tasks on a regular basis. If there are gaps then our office assistant Claire White will be completing these tasks.
- Our current payroll software (Payroll 987) provides the following functionality:-

1. Calculates who should be enrolled
2. Calculates pension contributions
3. Retains payroll related records as required by law
4. "Talks to" our pension provider of choice
5. Automatically enrols employees every three years

It does not:-

1. Issue mandatory communications

- We are going to be issuing the mandatory communications ourselves using the help and guidance that AE in a Box provides which lets us know when we need to send out the communications and which communications to send with links to template letters that we can use.
- Our payroll does everything apart from communications and this can be managed within the business therefore we will not be switching our payroll software.
- Our payroll does everything apart from communications and therefore middleware will not be needed to fill the gaps in auto enrolment functionality for our payroll.

Action timeline and taking action

- Nominate a contact – 17th September 2015
- Choosing a pension scheme - 17th September 2015
- Raising awareness about auto enrolment with our staff – 1st September 2015
- Agree contribution rates – 13th September 2015
- Will we be using postponement? – 15th January 2016
- Do we need additional software to help do worker assessments and keep compliant records? -6th November 2015
- Writing to staff who have/haven't been auto enroled – 16th March 2016
- Apply for Government Gateway ID – 17th March 2016

- Complete Declaration of compliance with The Pensions Regulator - 31st March 2016

Complying on an ongoing basis

We have signed up to receive the ongoing monthly emails from The Pensions Regulator so that we can be kept up to date with any changes that are made to the regulation.

Also we are signed up to AE in a Box which regularly updates its system to reflex any changes on regulation. It then produces tasks for us reflecting any changes that happen. We receive emails letting us know when tasks are due so that we complete everything on time. It also has tasks for things that need to be done on a monthly/weekly/ongoing basis.

Addendum ii

Employment Contracts and Pensions
By Vandana Dass - Davenports

It often surprises me how many businesses do not provide employment contracts to employees. This is due to a number of reasons, but mainly because businesses are too busy to focus on HR and employment matters.

For example, I speak to many employers who might have been trading for many years and have not issued contracts to their employees. Often this is because they do not feel the need to because they consider 'all of their employees are happy.'

I completely appreciate that the majority of employer/employee relationships are broadly positive. However it is important to remember that for a number of reasons this relationship can turn sour.

Therefore, it is advisable (and really important) for employers to always provide a written particulars of statement to their employees.

Whilst a contract of employment does not have to be in writing employees who have been employed for one month or more are entitled to a written statement of certain particulars of employment within two months of starting employment, under UK employment law under UK employment law This is often called a 'section 1 statement'.

Effectively the 'section 1 statement' must include all the terms and conditions governing the relationship between the employer and the employee and must include:

- The names of the employer and employee
- The date on which employment began, including any period of continuous employment with a previous employer.
- Rates of pay
- Hours of work including any overtime
- Terms relating to holidays, including public holidays and holiday pay
- The employee's job title or brief description of the work for which s/he employed
- Place of work, mobility clause and employer's address. If the employee is or may be required to work outside the UK for more than one month then this must be stated. It is also important to note that if an employee is based outside the UK then there are a number of additional points which the statement must set out.
- The rules relating to sickness and sick pay (including requirements for self-certification and details of payment during absence)
- Whether an employment is intended to be permanent, and if not, the period for which is it expected to last for (if it's a fixed term contract it will have an expiry date)
- Details of any notice period (there are specific additional rules around notice periods which is important for employers to understand)
- Disciplinary policies and procedures and
- Pension arrangements and other benefits that are provided as part of a pension scheme such as life insurance.

It is also important to remember that employees must be notified in writing of any changes to the above as soon as possible and in any event within one month of the change.

There are potentially expensive implications if an employer does not provide his employees with 'section 1 statement' or alternatively they have provided a statement which is inaccurate or incomplete.

Failure to provide the above to an employee means that employees may lodge a claim at the employment tribunal (employees may make a claim to an employment tribunal, within three months of the date of termination)and may be entitled to financial compensation if the employee has made another successful substantive claim.

It is important to remember that it is automatically unfair to dismiss an employee, regardless of length of service, because s/he has asked for a section 1 statement.

As we have already mentioned one of the particular details which must be included in a 'section 1 statement' are the particulars of pension arrangements.

The employer should be clear on the status of any new employee (that is, whether he is an eligible job holder under the automatic enrolment regulation) before finalising the pension clause(s) in the contract.

It is therefore fundamentally important for an employer who is approaching their staging date to have a process in place to manage their auto-enrolment duties.

Employers must also give employees certain basic information about their pensions under the rules established under both employment law and automatic enrolment regulation. It is advisable to include more information than this in the employment contract in order to protect the employer.

Therefore as an employer you may need to ensure that you include a statement of particulars of any terms relating to pensions and pension schemes in the written statement of particulars.

It is also important to remember that employees cannot be forced to join a pension scheme and any term that forces an employee to join a personal or occupational pension scheme is void.

So, whilst an employer is legally required to automatically enrol certain employees, these employees are entitled to opt-out.

Some employers include additional details of the pension terms (and more details in relation to the chosen employer's pension scheme) by referencing another document. However, if referring to another document, it must be reasonably accessible to the employees.

Employers should ensure that the wording used in the statement of particulars provides the employee only with a right to join whatever pension arrangements are operated by the employer from time to time. Employers should avoid using wording that gives the employee a right to receive pension benefits in a particular scheme at a particular level. If the employer does this, it will be difficult for it to make changes to the pension scheme at a later date.

In respect of the specific pension used employers should:

- Refer the employee to the scheme booklet that outlines the benefits provided under the scheme

- Avoid providing the employees with a contractual right for the employer to change the scheme or remove it in the future.
- Add a right for the employer to deduct any pension contributions payable to the scheme from the employee's salary either in the contract or in an application form for membership. If there is no written authority in place, this will be unauthorised deduction from the employee's wages.
- If a payment in lieu of notice (PILON) clause is included, this should only be in relation to the payment of basic salary and should, not include payment of pension benefits.

When a dispute arises between and employer and employee the starting point for establishing the intention of the parties is normally the written contract.

However, it is sometimes necessary to look beyond the written document, to the course of dealings between the parties and their subjective beliefs about what obligations they have entered into.

If the matter proceeds to an employment tribunal, the employment tribunal may imply a term, or may refuse to imply one, either of which may lead to one party finding that this is an unfair outcome.

It may seem obvious to point out, but clear drafting of a contract of employment is therefore vital to minimise the chances of a dispute between the parties about the true meaning of a term.

Addendum iii

The Automatic Enrolment Diaries

Revolution, Pace and why automatic enrolment is getting 14 times faster
First Published 18/02/2015

Since 2012 there's been thousands of employers who have complied successfully with auto enrolment.

However in the first 3 months of 2016 something revolutionary is happening…

In the last quarter of this year the number of employers who will be required to meet auto enrolment regulation is predicted to double.

I don't think the impact of this, for employers and the professionals who work with them, can be underestimated…

As the first quarter of 2016 starts it would have taken 3 and a half years for 100,000 odd employers to comply. In the early months of next year's it's estimated that an additional 110,000 employers will need to meet the new regulation.

This is a significant change of pace.

Over 100,000 employers complying in 3 and a half years compared to 110,000 having to comply in a three month period means that the velocity of the firms who have to meet the new regulation will increase 14 fold virtually immediately.

Also it's easy to forget that the firms who need to comply in the first 3 months of 2016 have a journey to make.

Typically in our experience the 'auto enrolment' project for most employers takes between 9 – 12 months.

This means that for the 100,000+ firms who need to comply near the end of this year ideally need to ensure they are starting to build a project plan, making some decisions and taking some action over the next couple of months.

The importance of preparing early has been made more pertinent by something which is also increasing in pace.

Employers are now having to pay the financial penalties of non-compliance more often than ever before.

So, if you're an employer who has been ignoring the impact of auto enrolment it's now time to understand that these obligations will be landing on your doorstep with increasing scale and pace soon.

If you're a financial professional looking at the best way to work with a number of employers finding the most efficient way to look after you and your professional connections clients is now more pertinent than ever.

and

If you're an accountant or payroll provider ensuring that you have an auto enrolment solution in place to deliver a service to all of your clients there's never going to be a better time to prepare (leaving this any later might put some of your clients at risk)

Why you need to be aware of the automatic enrolment non-compliance spike
First published on 29/11/16

Every few months the pension regulator releases a document. Now whilst I appreciate the not so snappily titled "Compliance and Enforcement quarterly bulletin" may not be at the top of everyone's reading list it does make for a fascinating read if you're engaged in helping employers comply with automatic enrolment.

Every time this document is released it reveals some interesting trends.

The first thing it shows is that, increasingly, the pension regulator is taking a lot more action on employers who don't comply with automatic enrolment..

The latest report looks at the period from the start of July to the end of September 2016.

In this 3 month period the pensions regulator used their various powers (which includes legal notices, fines and various other enforcement measures) a grand total of 19,825 times.

In total enforcement actions since automatic enrolment came into law and started to impact employers back in 2012 have been used 34,825 times.

This means that there have been as many enforcement actions taken against employers in the past three months than in the other four and a bit years automatic enrolment has applied to employers.

On face value that seems like a massive spike in non-compliance but actually it reflects the fact that the first large spike of employers had to comply at the start of this year.

These employers would have had a few months to complete their declarations of compliance (or not) and therefore it's clear that although the spike of non-compliance is concerning it is reflective of the fact that there has been a recent spike in employers needing to comply.

This brings me onto my second point...most employers seem to be complying successfully.

So far according to the pension minister there have been 250,000 + firms who have had to comply. Currently there have been 26,000 compliance notices issued.

Whilst over just over 10% non-compliance is still a relatively large percentage and the reality is that we don't know how many firms have said they have complied but missed certain parts of the process and the fact that we still have a million plus employers yet to comply on the whole employers have complied without a great deal of fuss.

However one other interesting thing in the report is clear...

The pensions regulator isn't too keen on excuses. In the latest copy of the compliance and enforcement report it has the following statement...

"The following do not amount to a reasonable excuse, whether for a failure to file a tax return or a failure to complete the declaration of compliance:

- you relied on someone else and they let you down

- you found the online system too difficult to use

- you didn't get a reminder

- you made a mistake

- you or a member of staff were ill."

So, whilst there has been a spike in automatic enrolment compliance but overall compliance broadly speaking remains pretty high the message from the pension regulator remains clear...

If employers don't comply the pensions regulator isn't afraid to take action.

An Auto Enrolment compliance story and why you might get so much right...but still not comply
first published on 13/09/16

One day I receive a call...

"I can't believe it Chris" said the director of a business.

"I spent some time to put in place a pension scheme, made sure my payroll could work with my pensions provider but I get this letter through the post saying I haven't complied and could be liable for a fine."

Whilst I couldn't give him an answer straight away without understanding a lot more about his business I felt I might have understood what the issue might have been and I found upon further investigation that my initial hunch had been correct.

You see this particular business owner had done loads right. He'd put in place a decent pension scheme, he'd got help from the people who ran his payroll. However the mistake he'd made was not fully understanding what he needed to do when it came to the regulation.

If you're an employer let me pass on a piece of friendly advice.

Take some time to understand what your obligations are under the automatic enrolment rules.

Understand what you need to do...but most importantly understand that there are tasks you need to complete which aren't directly pensions or payroll related (like reporting you've complied to the pensions regulator)

Now for employers who have the time and inclination to fully understand automatic enrolment it's possible for employers to comply directly and get everything sorted in the three areas employers need to action in, Pensions, Payroll AND Regulation.

...however for those employers who need help (and especially if you're one of them) they should consider getting support.

For smaller businesses with more limited budgets, our software service AE in a Box might be an appropriate approach.

Getting practical about automatic enrolment
First published on 09/08/16

"You see I've heard countless times about the fines and the rules Chris" said this lady I found myself chatting to last week "What I need to know now is the practical steps I need to take in order to comply"

It's not an unusual request. There is plenty of chat about automatic enrolment much of which involves the fines associated with getting it wrong, what some of the rules are and what complications need to be considered when complying with automatic enrolment.

However a decent number of employers want the same thing as the lady I spoke to last week...

They've heard enough about why they need to take action...now they just want to get on with the tasks at hand.

Of course there are a number of ways an employer can do this...

Some employers go through the process directly with some support on the payroll element from their accountant or payroll provider and guidance directly from the regulator.

Some employers prefer more bespoke support and are happy to pay consultancy fees to get this done (something we're constantly involved with at the minute)

and

Other employers want practical guidance on the jobs which need to be done in a systematic step by step way.

Now for employers who want to go alone with the pensions and regulatory element and with payroll support from their accountant or payroll provider we're not in a position to help.

However for every other employer we've got a solution which works.

For the employers who want consultancy services we can absolutely help with that and provide a service designed to be entirely bespoke to meet an employers needs.

and

For employers who need support to ensure they 'get the job done' both in terms of regulation and pension selection and want clarity on the tasks they need to do to comply there's AE in a Box...

Why financial penalties for automatic enrolment non-compliance can be easily avoided
First published on 11/08/16

As I write this there are a number of new surveys which are talking about the potential fines employed will incur by not complying with automatic enrolment over the next couple of years.

There is talk of 22 million pounds worth of fines, tens of thousands of employers being fined and hundreds of hours of time spent by employers trying to get automatic enrolment right.

Now at this point in time the reality is that we don't know what the final financial penalties are going to be incurred, how many employers are going to be penalised and how much time will be spent sorting stuff out.

However the reality is that the penalties for non-compliance are voluntary.

Employers don't have to pay fines for non-compliance by doing one simple thing...

Complying with automatic enrolment.

There's enough tools, support and resource available to help employers comply successfully.

This includes tools like AE in a Box

One thing is undeniable...

Whilst complying with automatic enrolment is a little easier than it was a few years ago it still takes time, effort and energy to ensure that employers comply well.

However whatever way you look at it the cost in either time or money to solve the automatic enrolment challenge is worth paying when compared to the financial penalties incurred, the hassle involved in rectifying issues and the potential reputational damage of getting it wrong.

So, if you're an employer (or help employers who run businesses) and need to comply (or help someone comply) soon please start sooner rather than later.

The fines might be easily avoided by simply complying...but could turn expensive if automatic enrolment is ignored.

ABOUT THE AUTHOR

Chris is the director of Cervello Financial Planning and AE in a Box and is also an experienced financial planner with over 18 years' experience in helping clients achieve their financial goals.

Chris specialises in working in conjunction with professionals including accountants and solicitors to help their clients with both their business and individual financial goals.

The majority of his clients are directors of owner managed businesses and Chris considers this to be his particular area of expertise.

However over the past few years Chris has specialised in helping firms of all sizes (ranging from 1,500 through to 30 employees) with the challenges they face whilst meeting the employer duties relating to automatic enrolment regulation.

Chris has also won numerous awards including the Unbiased Pension adviser of the year and 'group pension adviser of the year' at the FT Adviser life and pension awards.

Made in the USA
Charleston, SC
15 January 2017